Crossing a Bridge

Crossing a Bridge

The Master Plan for Making Later-in-Life Living
Decisions that Preserve Your Dignity and Peace of
Mind

Raleigh R. Lee

Ivey Gate Press

Brookhaven, Georgia

Ivey Gate Press

4090 Ivey Gate

Brookhaven, Georgia 30341

www.crossingabridge.com
raleigh@crossingabridge.com
800.861.1457

Publisher's Note: Some material in this book is published with the permission of the SRES® Council.

Crossing a Bridge / Raleigh R. Lee. -- 1st ed.

ISBN-13: 9781984296795

ISBN-10: 1984296795

Contents

Disclaimer

This book is not a substitute for the medical advice of physicians, tax advice from your tax professional, or legal advice from your lawyer. Consult a specialized practitioner in these matters.

A diligent effort has been made to ensure that the information in this book is accurate and complete. However, the author and publisher do not guarantee the accuracy of the information, text, and graphics contained within the book due to the rapidly changing nature of science, research, or known and unknown facts. The author and publisher do not hold any responsibility for errors, omissions or contrary interpretation of the subject matter here. This book is presented solely for informational purposes.

Use caution and always consult your accountant, lawyer or professional advisor before acting on this or any information related to a lifestyle change, your business, or finances. You alone are the variable and are accountable for the results you get in your life, and by reading this book, you agree not to hold the author or publisher liable for your decisions, actions or outcomes, at any time, under any circumstance.

The Ideal Audience for this Book

- Baby Boomers whose homes no longer suit them

- Anyone looking for help in making later-in-life living/retirement choices

- Younger people trying to help older loved ones make decisions to improve their living conditions

The Goal of the Book

I designed this book as a pathway for making your best later-in-life living choices. I want to expand your knowledge of how life stages and situations have an impact on your thinking. I also want to give you some ideas for how to deal with them and connect you to a network of resources for help.

Many of the choices made later in life lead to real estate dealings. However, this book is not about buying and selling real estate so much. It's about creating smart living outcomes. Those decisions could focus on retirement, aging in place, assisted living, or other options.

I hope this book is . . .

- a realistic and practical take on complex issues that rise above truisms

- insightful with strategies that are easy to read and to understand

- a presentation of easy to digest, simple choices in matters that are most relevant to you

- a chapter-by-chapter journey structured according to step-by-step decisions

- a segmented flow so that you can start at any chapter most vital to you

- reflective of real-life scenarios that give hope and practical suggestions

- first-rate research and facts supported by steps leading to great decisions

- without annoying and repetitive examples

What You Will Learn from This Research

- How to Understand and Get Along with Other Age Groups

- How to Prepare Yourself for 21st Century Retirement

- What It Means to 'Age in Place' and How to Do It Safely and Comfortably

- Understanding the Choices for Independent Living

- Making the Best Decisions About Assisted Living

- Choosing the Best Financing Options for Your Living Choices

- Making the Most of the Tax Benefits in Real Estate Transactions

- Making the Right Legal Decisions About Your Estate

- How to Avoid Abuse, Family Disputes, Schemes, and Scams Later in Life

Foreword

The old saying goes, "I'll cross that bridge when I get to it." Don't do that. When you must make later-in-life living decisions, crossing the bridge when you get to it might be too late.

You should know ahead of time what the bridge looks like, what obstacles it presents to you, and how to cross it successfully. That's what this book is all about.

Plan while you can. If you don't, someone else might plan for you; and you might not like their decisions.

Inside these pages, you'll find a strategy. You will discover alternatives and options that you might not have thought of or didn't know existed. The plan is far-reaching and supported by sound research. It is not all-inclusive because the choices can fill volumes rather than just one book. What is lacking here, you can find through the list of resources in the back of the manual.

I was born in 1942, so I've crossed a few bridges myself. I know that I have others in front of me, and I want to navigate them all with dignity and peace of mind. My training as a Seniors Real Estate Specialist® opened my eyes to the complexities of later-in-life living choices and set me on a mission to open the eyes of others facing these options. In fact, my content draws extensively from the SRES® training manual, which is the most complete source on this subject I have found.

As you go through the first five chapters, you may sense the personal touch from my experience. The sections on financing options, tax matters, and legal issues are not so subjective. They reflect what is available, in our codes, and lawful today. I'm not a financial expert, accountant, or lawyer. Therefore, it is difficult to give this examination a personal touch. However, I have simplified the language commonly used to discuss these issues so that they may be more readily understood.

I hope you gain from the research as I have presented it. I learned a lot from conducting it.

Raleigh R. Lee
REALTOR®, Seniors Real Estate Specialist®, ABR®, CRS

Preface

As we pulled out of the parking lot, it hit me like a shot between the eyes, and I couldn't hold it back. I started weeping like a 2-year-old; I was 58.

My mother, in the passenger seat beside me, treated me like a baby at that moment. She comforted me with the same tenderness I had received from her all my life.

"Don't worry," she said, "I'll be all right." I believed her.

I believed her because, together, we had just made a delightful discovery. My tears came from bliss. I was overcome with emotion as the sense of relief overpowered me.

She turned 93 the day I cried in the car. However, we started this journey when she was about 85 and still mowing her lawn with a push mower. It wasn't until then that she started thinking about what she might do 'when she got old.'

We first visited Magnolia Manor then. She liked it, but turned down the offer to move in, saying she didn't want to "live with a bunch of old people."

My mother much preferred the scene from her little beach cottage. The thunder of motorcycles and crazy Tybee Island parades coming down her street close to the ocean tickled her.

She was able to walk a 10K race at that age, but I became concerned still. I would sometimes find her sitting alone in a darkened room almost, maybe fully asleep when I visited. Sometimes she didn't hear my arrival. I would startle her when I planted a kiss on her cheek as she sat there snoozing. That worried me.

So, we started our search for some help. At one time we hired a local in-home caregiver, but that didn't work out well. Too much personality clash, I think. Fortunately, the beach community was tight; so, there was some neighborhood help. However, Mama always felt guilty about that.

We visited 'nursing homes.' That frightened and depressed us both at the time. We did as much as we could without the resources available to us now through the internet.

Nothing appealed to either of us. No alternative was better than staying put and growing older . . . and older . . . and older. However, reality raised its ugly head. We had to do something at some point.

My mother was a constant companion of reality. She was a practical person.

One day we stood watching ostriches and buffalos and goats at a roadside convenience store (strange, I know, but true) on a highway between Atlanta and Savannah. When we started to hit the road again, she stumbled a bit from the South Georgia heat as she got in the car. Then she said, "You know, Raleigh, I think I need to quit driving."

That was it! That was the beginning of some serious thinking about her old age. That was when we returned to Magnolia Manor to reconsider her moving there.

"Mama, I broke down because I thought that place was just great," I said after I regained my composure in the driveway. "Well, you ought to cry when you're sad – not when you're happy," she said. Her companionship with reality popped up.

"I'm just so glad that you've decided to live there." The food was good. Her apartment had a little balcony that overlooked a lake bordered by southern live oaks draped with Spanish moss. The people were nice. Moreover, there was no smell. I was overjoyed.

She lived there for four years until her balance failed her. The result was a broken hip and a trip to the hospital, where she swiftly declined. I said goodbye to her at her bedside, and she said she was "ready to go." Then I went outside in the hallway and cried again.

She lingered there, so they transported her to Hospice Savannah; and we braced ourselves for her death. However, some force had other ideas. She rallied.

Now we were faced with more decisions. Hospice kicks you out unless you show signs of dying within a reasonable period. It was clear at this point that Mama wasn't ready to die yet, so we had to make other choices.

I began to search Savannah for a skilled nursing facility I could stomach. The clock was ticking at Hospice. They moved Mama into Azalealand Nursing Home.

***

For more than ten years I helped my mother make the transition from aging in place . . . to caregiver support . . . to assisted living . . . to a skilled nursing facility . . . to her final resting place on a scenic bluff of the Wilmington River in Savannah, Georgia. However, there's more to our story.

About 15 years later I woke up with a seven-inch wound in the middle of my chest, coughing uncontrollably and unable to talk. My throat was as dry as the Atacama Desert. I wondered how dry my mother's throat was as she starved herself to death in her bed at Azalealand.

My wife, Janice, told me that the first thing I said after the surgery was "That wasn't as bad as I thought it would be." The next day I suffered diabolical pain of biblical proportions, and it continued without relief for about three weeks.

Six months of dealing with the agony and lingering effects of open heart surgery embedded in me a firm awareness of the pain others may feel – for any reason, but especially for aging reasons. It also gave me a sense of urgency to plan for the time when I had to cross the bridge from independence to assisted living and instilled in me a commitment to help others with age-related issues.

Two life-changing incidents, 15 years apart, brought me to this place. These two events caused me to educate myself about the options for later-in-life living choices. I became an expert in these issues through training and research, and wrote this book.

Don't wait for a life-changing event to change your life. Plan while you can.

Chapter 1

How to Get Along with Age Groups

Why is it vital to start with this subject? Understanding each other is key to good communication. First-rate communication is basic to getting things done, reaching goals, and fixing problems.

We often need to remind ourselves of who we are. It's helpful to know what others think about us when we try to work with each other and team up on projects.

So, in this spirit, we start here.

These are the most common issues misjudged about Baby Boomers. Until I got older myself, I might have believed some of the myths that exist about aging. I finally began to dry off behind the ears and work with people about my age. Old age allowed me to see the truths more clearly.

Geezers – Myths and Truths

Myth: Old People Are All the Same.

Reality: The range of interests and experiences of youth and middle age is no less present in mature years. In fact, older people are more diverse in key ways than younger ones. We all know someone who is a "youthful" 80 or an "old" 50. Health is a vital factor in aging, and inborn makeup plays a role in both how quickly we age and what ailments we get.

Other factors are also at work on us such as learning, climate, activity level, diet, and social networks. We can't control the setting into which we're born or what we go through in childhood. Our actions and choices as adults shape the course of life. Also, everyone's life events are unique.

Myth: Families "Dump" Kinfolks into Nursing Homes

Reality: Nursing homes are a last resort for most people. It doesn't seem like it, but less than 5% of older folks live in nursing homes. For the most part, families give in-home care with little or no outside support until the time of a crisis. Services that aid elders to stay in their own homes or with loved ones are the first choice.

***

Myth: Old Equals Sick and Laid Up

Reality: Research says that more than half of people surveyed at all age levels rated their health as good to excellent. Boomers, though, are less likely to assess their health as very good or excellent than older groups at the same life stage.

In a study by the National Bureau of Economic Research, Boomers reported more pain, chronic complaints, alcohol and substance abuse, and psychiatric problems. Boomers also report higher stress levels than earlier groups – from jobs, finances, and caring for parents and children. The study findings raise the question of whether the Baby Boomers are going into senior years in worse shape than prior generations.

While ill health rates among the 65+ population have declined in the last 20 years, the trend may reverse if the Baby Boomers retire with more chronic and disabling health ailments. On the other hand, Boomers – the "forever young" age group – are more health conscious and have higher hopes than earlier generations.

***

Myth: Old People Are Lonely and Slowly Withdraw

Reality: Although the number of casual contacts may decline, mature and elder adults have close friends and networks to the same degree that younger people do. Dealings with family and friends are a vital part of pleasure with life. Keeping ties with friends, family, and the village is a weighty reason for the desire to age in place. Only a small fraction of elders is on bad terms with family, mostly due to long-standing falling-out. Most 50+ adults are members of the family network, see their children weekly, or have frequent phone contact. But, for reasons of privacy and autonomy, most elders express a desire not to live with their children.

Transportation is a central factor in keeping up social involvement as well as gaining access to basic services and even needed health treatment. The physical, mental, and financial elements that make it hard for elders to drive also make it tough to use public transportation.

***

Myth: Older People Are Richer, Poorer Than Young People.

Reality: Social Security has reduced the number of older people living in scarcity. In the 1960s, 45 percent of seniors lived in hardship, and only 60 percent received Social Security. The elder poverty level dropped by 10 percent by the 1990s. Ninety-three percent of them received Social Security payments. Many mature adults are cash-poor and house-rich. For a lot of seniors, their homes account for most of their net wealth.

***

Myth: Older People Are More Likely to Be Victims of a Crime.

Reality: According to the U.S. Department of Justice, older people are less likely to be victims of crime than young people. Property crimes are by far the most frequent. However, safety and fear of crime are chief factors in choosing a place to live. When older adults are the target of crimes, they are more likely to incur severe damage. They are also more likely to face crooks who are strangers.

***

Myth: Every Retired Person Wants to Live in Florida.

Reality: The geographic dispersal of old folks follows the same pattern as the total population. The most crowded states are also home to the chief ratios of older people.

Eight out of 10 Americans live in metro areas, and so does the older population. About one quarter live in the central city. Metro elders cite access to cultural and learning events as prime influences. They also value the transportation, healthcare, and shopping in metro areas that would be hard to find in small towns or rural settings. The tradeoff for big city life, though, could be a higher cost of living.

***

Myth: Older People Do Not Use Technology.

Reality: Geezers are connected. Using email and reading news updates rank first and second as the most common online events. Social media is quickly catching up. Some older people may favor face-to-face or the phone, but for many checking emails is part of the daily routine.

According to the Pew Research Center, 34% of adults aged 65 and older used social networks like Facebook in 2016. The number was 64% for those in the 50-64 age range. I think Facebook users in both of those age groups have grown in a big way since that study.

How do older folks use social media? They reconnect with people from the past. They reach out for support online, especially those dealing with chronic health complaints.

They keep in touch with far-flung family members. For "snowbirds" and those who are always on the go, email or social media may be the best way to stay in touch.

More than half of American workers aged 55-59 use computers all or most of the time in their jobs. High-tech Boomers regard a Web connection as one of life's basic needs.

The Six Living Generations

Name	Born	Characteristics
G.I. Generation	1901 – 1924	<ul><li>energetic</li><li>patriotic</li><li>courageous</li><li>loyal</li><li>community oriented</li><li>hardworking</li><li>team players</li><li>respect for authority</li></ul>
Silent Generation	1925 – 1945	<ul><li>cautious</li><li>conformist</li><li>risk averse</li><li>unimaginative</li><li>industrious</li><li>prudent</li><li>unquestioning of authority</li><li>the "beat" generation</li></ul>

Name	Born	Characteristics
Baby Boomers	1946 – 1964	▪ ambitious ▪ optimistic ▪ individualistic ▪ immediate gratification ▪ hardworking ▪ competitive ▪ materialistic ▪ forever young
Generation X	1965 – 1976	▪ skeptical ▪ latchkey kids ▪ isolated ▪ cynical ▪ entrepreneurial ▪ independent ▪ quality of life/family before career ▪ self-reliant ▪ pragmatic ▪ reluctant to commit

Name	Born	Characteristics
Millennials, Generation Y	1977 – 1994	<ul><li>empathetic with elders</li><li>sheltered</li><li>tolerant</li><li>sensitive to multiculturalism</li><li>hopeful</li><li>over-scheduled</li><li>multitaskers</li><li>short attention span</li></ul>
Generation Z	1995 –	<ul><li>technology adept</li><li>connected</li><li>introverted</li><li>short attention span</li><li>individualistic</li><li>impatient</li><li>communicate online</li></ul>

Source: SRES® Student Manual V 2.2

Understanding How We Age

There are times when something new happens to my body or mind, and I wonder what's going on. Often, I have to look it up to understand these changes.

There are also times when I'm surprised or dismayed when others around me don't seem to know or care about what I'm going through. The fact that I can no longer contort my body to turn the water off under my sink escapes them. They don't pitch in to help me change a light that I can't reach without a ladder because they don't realize I've lost some of my sense of balance.

Gaining some grasp of these limits helps me cope and place a value on the new thing. These briefs that follow might, in turn, be helpful to someone making the later-in-life decisions discussed in this book.

Mental Ability

The skills to learn, adapt, adjust, and be creative are quite sturdy throughout life. However, interests and drives shape people. The habit of lifelong learning supports mental power.

The ability to recall names and events may decline, but long-term memory is quite strong. Mild cognitive impairment (MCI) doesn't hinder actions of daily living or social contact like Alzheimer's.

Vision

As we age, being both near and far-sighted is more and more common. Low eyesight is more widespread than complete blindness. Subtle color changes may become less distinct. At night, glare from oncoming traffic's headlights and wet streets can make driving difficult.

Hearing

Hearing damage usually starts with a loss in the higher register tones. It works its way down until it reaches the tone-range of speech.

Health

By age 70, almost everyone has one or more of seven common chronic health problems: arthritis, high blood pressure, heart disease, diabetes, lung disease, stroke, or cancer.

Height

Posture, spinal alignment and compression, and falling arches all can cause decreased height.

Weight

Weight rises in men until mid-50s and in women until late 60s. It then slowly declines for both genders.

Temperature

We become more exposed to heat stroke, hypothermia, and drying out. Keeping a healthy temperature and blood pressure becomes less likely.

TakeAways

- Understand who you are and how others may see you.

- Show this research to loved ones who might be helping but who misunderstand you.

Chapter 2

Prepare Yourself for 21st Century Retirement

Baby Boomers started reaching age 65 at the rate of 10,000 every day in January 2011. By 2030 all Boomers will reach that age milestone. They have reshaped every phase of life from childhood onward. It looks like their outlooks and hopes will write a new story of retirement.

Many Boomers intend to age in place, but their housing needs will change as they grow older. Will they see their homes as an asset and tap into the equity to support their retirement years? Or will they echo the mindsets of the former age groups who would never put their homes at risk?

How the Retirement Model is Changing

President Franklin Roosevelt signed the Social Security Act in 1935. The people who wrote it planned to offer a secure retirement for the few years between the end of working life and death. At the time, standard life spans in America were 58 years for men and 62 years for women. Actuaries assumed that disease would claim the lives of many before they were eligible for payments.

Advances in health care and treatment of life-curbing ailments have lengthened lives. The average North American born in 1960 lives to the age of at least 73 years. Preventive medicine, diet, and training add healthy years in middle and later life, not just putting off years of infirm old age. Retirement is now the "second half of life." It is a time for an "encore career" – reinvention and redefinition.

Retirement Attitudes – Mature Generations Versus Boomers

The mature (GI and Silent) folks built age-restricted and active adult communities. They designed them for their age brackets. The ideal retirement for them was a time to quit work for a life of endless leisure in a warm climate. They designed most of the customs in place today – health care delivery, government programs and prospects such as age milestones – for this concept of retirement.

But, when it comes to age-constrained housing, less than half (48 percent) of Baby Boomers say they would think about it. And housing choice is not the only way the Boomers are re-thinking things.

They favor more of an open setting with part-time work or scattered periods of leisure and work. When asked why, mental stimulus and challenge outranked making money.

They also want contact with people other than Boomers. The link to younger people helps this forever-young crowd stay that way. The National Association of Realtor's research study of Baby Boomers and real estate found that the median age at which they plan to stop working is 70 years. Many Boomers never intend to quit working. Not surprisingly, those who feel the least prepared to quit plan to stay at work the longest.

Many of today's current retirees are returning to the workplace. Almost a quarter of retirees born between 1933 and 1937 are re-entering the workforce. Many cite financial reasons. They also want to stay busy and network with others.

Boomers feel that their parents' ideal retirement is not only high-priced, but it is dreary. They are still thinking it out, but Boomers will force customs and old models to adapt.

The Impact of Economic Recession

The Great Depression touched many in the mature generations (GI and Silent). For them, this last downturn we lived through was nothing new. They already knew how to cope with lean times. But they also went through the long bull markets of 1953-1959 and 1981-1989 and post-war good fortune without global competition. Many of them also had generous pension plans.

Boomers have gone through two long-lasting bear markets during their peak earning years. There has also been some lasting market volatility in a few sectors. Some Boomers are still trying to get their fiscal houses in order.

This last slump hit at a time when there was less time to recover money-wise for those closest to retirement. The downturn that began in 2008 might not have had much impact on the retirement plans of Boomers because their dreams were already modest. They were planning to work during retirement anyway.

Special Retirement Challenges

The Sandwich Generation Factor

You may be a victim of the "sandwich" generation. Many children depend on their parents for money even as they move into middle age. If that is the case with you and *your* parents also depend on you, you have the "sandwich" factor.

What's the likely reason for most of this? It's the high costs for college and burden of school loan debt for many young adults. Some Boomers think about moving to adult-living places to stop adult children from "boomeranging" back home to live.

Almost a third of Boomers help their parents with money. About 70 percent of their parents (one or both) are still living. Although these elderly parents may be in better health and better off than former generations, they are still likely to rely on their children for help with caregiving and household errands.

How to Survive the Sandwich Generation

- **Engage intergenerational daycare**: These services have adult care programs as well as child-care programs in one center.

- **Practice Self-Care**: Make sure you get exercise, proper nutrition, sleep and regular doctor appointments.

- **Save Time While Updating Family**: Give updates to everyone at once to lower your stress level. You can use Google Drive or *Lotsa Helping Hands* to create a document or spreadsheet that everyone has access to and can update.

- **Share the Load**: Stop stressing and start delegating.

- **Get Some Help**: Find a senior care aide to help your mom while you take your son to soccer practice. Hire a babysitter for your kids while you take your dad to the doctor.

- **Talk to Your Employer**: Talk to your boss about switching to a more open schedule. Or see if your company offers child or senior care.

- **Prioritize What Matters**: Make a list of all the things you think need to be done. Then rank them. What can you cut out? How can you lessen your workload each day?

- **Be Selfish**: Allow yourself to do at least one thing for yourself every day, just because you enjoy it.

- **Lean on Support**: Talk to other family members and friends about what you're dealing with. Or join a local support group.

Grandparents Raising Grandchildren

Six million grandparents raise their grandchildren. That's about 8 percent of the children in the United States. They step into a childcare role because their adult offspring can't care for their kids or are absent. Each case is unique, but almost all involve painful family choices and settings.

Grandparents may feel better equipped to parent their children's children than their own. They may also believe the practice helps them stay active and gives a sense of purpose. But there is no doubt that childcare a second time around is physically and emotionally stressful.

Late-life parenting tasks can strain marriages and other relationships. They can add a financial burden as the grandparents try to prepare for retirement. And housing can be a problem if gramps lives in a community that doesn't allow lengthy stays for youngsters.

The AARP has a helpful guide for grandparents who raise their grandchildren. Go to their website at *aarp.org/relationships/friends-family/info-08-2011/grandfamilies-guide-getting-started.html* for that information.

Single Retirees

More than one-third (37 percent) of Baby Boomers are on their own. They've either stayed single, gotten divorced, split-up, or been widowed.

How to Thrive as a Single Retiree

- **Cultivate a support network.** Find people who can check in on you and help with tasks such as driving you to appointments and helping with shopping and chores.

- **Build your social network.** Devote more effort to making and keeping friendships. Websites such as the *Osher Lifelong Learning Institute, Road Scholar,* and *SeniorNet* can help you find programs of interest to you.

- **Consider alternative living arrangements.** Here are two options for living measures that can give support and delay the need to move to an assisted living facility:

  - *Co-housing communities* are intentional communities of private homes clustered around a shared space. Each attached or single-family home has traditional features, including a private kitchen. Shared spaces may include a large kitchen and dining area, laundry and recreational spaces. Neighbors commit to being part of a village for everyone's shared benefit. They plan and manage community activities and shared spaces. They also share resources like tools and lawnmowers.

- *Shared housing* is two or more unrelated adults sharing a home. The old Golden Girls TV show was a prime example. Several websites can aid those seeking house sharing deals by finding those who have space to offer. They include the *National Shared Housing Resource Center* and the *Cohousing Association of the United States*. These sites also have resources for how to set up and manage successful house sharing deals.

- **Be willing to travel solo**. If you have some doubts about touring alone, begin slowly. Start with day trips in your car or weekend trips to a nearby city. Cruise ships and group tours are options worth thinking about.

Home – Asset or Anchor?

Eight out of 10 older Americans own a home and of those more than two-thirds own their homes free and clear with no loan debt. How much equity is in *your* home? And to what extent would you use it to fund your retirement?

The mature generations see their homes as the last place they would ever give up or risk. Boomers are more accustomed to seeing their homes as part of a portfolio of assets. They may be more likely to take cash out of home equity through a line of credit or loan.

Which one are you? How do you feel about this option?

What Is the Ideal Retirement Setting?

When budding retirees are asked to describe the ideal setting to give up work, a suburb, small town, or rural setting in the South or West is the most favored. Research from these states reports that many of the newly retired arrivals are active adults from Eastern and Midwestern states. For these retirees, the significant factors in choosing a location are:

- Low cost of living

- Near family

- Access to good healthcare

- Safety

- Better climate

- Near a lake, river, or ocean

Overall, Boomers are planning to stay close to home with almost two-thirds expecting to still be in the same state. In some cases, with steady work as an economic need, nearness to firms who hire older workers may become a gripping factor for choosing a retirement site.

Finding the Good Life – Money, Meaning, and Meds

The MetLife Mature Marketing Institute asked the question: What creates the *Good Life*? All age groups replied that three things were central: money (fiscal well-being), meaning (time with family and friends), and medicine (good physical and mental health). The Good Life has a sense of purpose, defined as:

- Vision – clarity about the path to the Good Life

- Focus – aware and fixed on the most important things

People aged 45-74 report a greater clarity of vision and focus than those aged 25-44. The older group focuses more on meaning-laden events. Finding purpose is a constant quest rather than a one-time trip to an exotic land.

Speaking of Exotic Lands

If you're thinking about joining the expat community, you're part of a growing crowd. If you get serious about it, you should Google the subject. Citing the 'best places' here wouldn't be responsible because you should seek out the latest research.

The number of Americans retiring outside the U.S. grew 17 percent between 2010 and 2015. As of 2017, about 400,000 American retirees lived abroad. That number is likely to increase over the next ten years as more Baby Boomers retire.

The people that research this retirement alternative crunch data and personal insights for a lot of categories. They look at things like cost of living, visas & residence, fitting in, and climate. From this data, they compile their rankings.

Even the *International Living* folks don't think you should move to a foreign country for retirement just because it scores well in their (or anyone else's) ranking, though. Before moving, you should profile yourself about what you want in a place. Find out what you must have to live. Then, be sure any place you're thinking about is a fit.

And before making a lasting move to a foreign country, try it out for as long as you can. See what it's like to be there – not just on vacation, but long enough to set up Internet access and open a bank account.

I add one other warning about the *International Living* rankings: The political and economic climate in the U.S. can change a great deal at any time. Such changes could, in turn, affect the lure of some countries as retirement havens.

What If You Want/Need to Keep Working?

Could there be a silver lining for Boomers' continued employment? Retirees who go on to work also continue to pay taxes. They may relieve some of the financial burdens predicted to crush the Social Security system. You could be part of a solution rather than part of a problem.

Retirement Resources

There are a growing number of sources to help people find their way in the new retirement landscape. The AARP has started a project called *Life Reimagined for Work*. It bills itself as "a think-and-do lab . . . to help people reimagine their lives." The project helps connect people with concerns looking to hire skilled employees. It also hosts LinkedIn group talks on work and life issues. It features stories about people who have gone on to fruitful second, third and fourth acts.

April is now *Encore Entrepreneurial Mentor Month*, according to the AARP. If you're over 50, you can go to workshops and forums and take free online courses at their site during April.

Jan Hively, at age 75, co-founded *Shift*. It is a nonprofit networking group that helps people find pleasing and sustainable work later in life.

And then there is *Encore.org*, a nonprofit dedicated to pushing "second acts for the greater good" for those over 50.

Silver Collar Cities

According to the US Census Bureau's American Community Survey, there are 10 "silver collar cities." So-called *Silver Collar Cities* are where a lot of workers keep working past retirement age. And a common theme is a lot of government employers and schools as well as retired white-collar execs who become consultants. In summary, this list shows where they are and how much of the workforce are retirees who keep working.

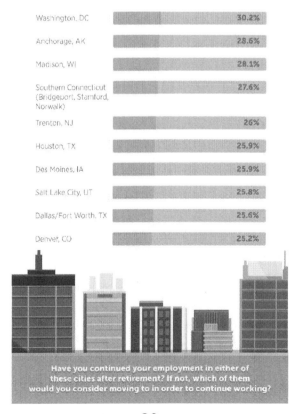

City	%
Washington, DC	30.2%
Anchorage, AK	28.6%
Madison, WI	28.1%
Southern Connecticut (Bridgeport, Stamford, Norwalk)	27.6%
Trenton, NJ	26%
Houston, TX	25.9%
Des Moines, IA	25.9%
Salt Lake City, UT	25.8%
Dallas/Fort Worth, TX	25.6%
Denver, CO	25.2%

Have you continued your employment in either of these cities after retirement? If not, which of them would you consider moving to in order to continue working?

29

What explains why these areas are called Silver Collar Cities? More than 15% of Americans aged 62 or older work. In Washington, D.C. that number is more than 30%.

Here's why:

Joel Reaser (a senior vice president at the National Older Worker Career Center in Arlington, VA) said: "It's all the retired federal workers." Federal workers don't just retire after their public-service career is over at around age 53. Instead, they keep working as consultants or find other occupations. And later they might retire.

Anchorage, Alaska is a constant leader in over-62 workers with about 29% employed. Once again, the government seems to be the reason. According to the Alaska Labor Department, state and local government hired the highest percentage of Alaskans aged 55 to 64. Their schools reported as much as 15% of their workforce was 65 or older. When you think about it, many people who do quit working after age 62 move to warmer climates.

The truth is, older folks can't endure grueling work like digging ditches or pounding nails. But government jobs can employ workers for decades after average retirement age. Some in a program that puts about 700 retirees to work at federal agencies are in their 90s.

Reaser said that "There's a very large number of retired federal workers that consult and work for federal agencies." The Department of Defense, he said, "has one of the largest concentrations of contractors."

Beyond that, there's the urban factor. There is a contrast between urban areas and the rest of the country in this study. Census Bureau figures show that 183 metro areas with populaces above 250,000 employed 21% of the people aged 62 or older. That compares to 17% nationwide. Those numbers ranged from 30% in Washington to 4% in several Puerto Rican cities.

Why is this so? Six of the top 10 cities with more than 10,000 workers over the age of 62 were state capitals. Hence, the pull of government. All, except the Bridgeport-Stamford area in Connecticut, had job loss rates among retirement-age workers who want to stay in the workforce below the national average of 9.1%.

What Does Weather Have to Do with the Trend to Continue Working?

Except for Houston and Dallas, all were north of the Mason-Dixon line. Miami and most other Florida cities showed 20% or less of retirement-age people still working. The trend held in retiree-heavy Arizona as well. Apparently, retirement means retirement in those sunny locales.

It all comes down to this: Would you be happy moving (if you must) to one of these metro areas to continue working? Following this plan could be your solution to the fears about your age.

TakeAways

- The concept of retirement has changed, and that has opened some new prospects for you.

- If the "Sandwich" factor, grandkids, being single, or home value hinders your retirement there are answers.

- You can find your ideal retirement setting based on sound research, but you must know what you want and need.

- There are lots of resources available if you plan to work into your retirement.

Chapter 3

If You Want to Age in Place, Make a Plan

In this section, we look at choosing to stay put or move to a new housing situation. Some hurdles to making this choice are clear, but others are subtle. The notion of giving up a long-time home can crush you even when looking forward to making a change.

What is your concept of aging in place? Is it to live safely, without help, and at ease in your own home and the cozy settings of a caring village?

Just bear in mind that aging in place is not a passive event. It doesn't result from merely staying put and adding up the years. According to AARP research, 8 out of 10 adults will face future special housing needs.

Fruitful aging in place is a process. You must take stock of current and future needs, think through the options, evaluate the house and area, and make plans. The process starts with asking the question:

What will it take for you to age well in this home and community?

Start Your Plan with These Thoughts

For many, where they live at retirement is the place they want to live out their lives. Does this mean that mature adults don't move to new homes or communities? Some move before reaching an age or life-stage milestone.

Second-home owners may choose their vacation homes for aging in place. Another option is to move to a future retirement dwelling and commute from there before quitting work for good.

The choice of where and how to age in place depends mainly on health and support needs. We'll look at how you can adapt your home for aging in place and help you find answers to make that shift well. Let's begin by looking at two aspects of the plan:

- **Aging in the community:** Staying in a neighborhood you're used to but in a more fitting home. Or moving to a community that has a safe setting and needed aids and help, or moving closer to the family.

- **Aging in the home:** Staying in the current house, accessing support services, and reworking the building as needs change.

A plan for aging in place is not a plan for advanced old age or illness. It is a set of ideas for keeping control of your environs and quality of life. When family members join in planning, they have a chance to voice concerns, work through real-world issues, and think about their future roles. They also learn your wishes and likings.

Where Are You on the Planning Scale?

It may help to think of an aging-in-place plan as a scale based on health and support needs. Where you fit on the gamut shows present and future actions, primary concerns, and how quickly you need to make choices. We should tie this scale to health, mobility, care, and service needs, not certain ages.

Stage 1 - No Urgent Needs

There is time to think ahead, research options, create plans, and discuss choices with family members. Simple universal design home changes can improve self-contained living and prevent bad mishaps and falls. This stage may involve a planned move to a second home or active adult community. Your area should enable you to take part in group events, volunteer causes, and stay involved in an active lifestyle.

Stage 2 - Progressive or Chronic Health Conditions

Changes in life and health conditions demand home modifications or a move to a more fitting living layout. Although not needed now, a slow sequence of ailments makes changes bound to happen. There is time to research care options, move to a more suitable home or closer to the family. Your community should support independent living, afford easy access to health care sources, and offer crisis response.

Stage 3 - Urgent Needs, Sudden Changes, Advanced Conditions

A sudden change in health or life events calls for quick modifications to the home and maybe the living setting. Progressive ailments reach advanced stages and need full-time care. Home modifications are needed to allow caution and maintain safety. A full-time care provider or a move to a medically oriented care resource may be needed. Your area should support long-term medical care.

Make a SAFE Plan for Aging in Place

When is a house, or community, fit for aging in place and when is it right to ponder a move to another home or neighborhood? Remember these four factors when making your decisions:

1. Safety   2. Access

3. Fits Needs   4. Ease of Use

Factor	In the Home	In the Community
Safety	Does the home have features that present risks, such as dim lighting, steep stairs, no handrails, clutter, frayed wiring, or structural problems?	Does the area seem unsafe? Are people afraid to leave their homes? Is the community fading?
Access	Are family and friends close by or far away? Will you be cut off and trapped in the home? Is entry awkward for the home or other areas? Are cabinets, closets, appliances, and storage handy?	Are shopping and services nearby? Can you quickly access vital services – grocery store, pharmacy, house of worship, medical facilities, or bank – without driving?

Factor	In the Home	In the Community
Fits Needs	Does the house still fit your needs? Can you handle the repair and upkeep of an older home?	Does the community give support for aging in place? Is the climate okay year-round?
Ease of Use	Are doors and hallways big enough for a walker or wheelchair? Can home features be added or changed?	Does the community setup promote ease of movement?

Source: SRES® Student Manual V 2.2

Aging in Place: The Community

What makes a community a right place to age in place? AARP offers the following list of features that support independent living for older adults:

- Well-run community centers, leisure centers, parks, and other areas where people can mingle and take part in public meetings and events

- Volunteer prospects

- Steady public transport. Safe and handy transportation options offered, such as rides from friends or family

- Safe sidewalks that connect places people want to go to on foot

- Roads designed for safe driving with clear-cut signage and marked traffic stops and crosswalks for people on foot

- Range of housing options, with housing within your means

Naturally Occurring Retirement Communities

Not all Baby Boomer communes are planned developments. Some happen logically as long-time residents of a neighborhood age in place. About one in four mature adults live in a naturally occurring retirement community (NORC). Except for the age of the tenants, there are seldom any other central features. NORCs happen in small towns, suburbs, and rural settings. They can be a community, an apartment building, or a section of a neighborhood and are more and more common in rural areas.

Aging in Place: The Home

What makes a home right for aging in place? MetLife and the National Association of Homebuilders surveyed aged 55+ households about the preferences for home features, comforts, and services. Survey participants replied with the following choices:

· Suburban or near suburban location

· Single-family detached home

· One-level, two-car garage

· 3-4 bedrooms, 2-3 bathrooms

· Open kitchen and family room

· Separate living room

· Median size of 1,900 square feet

About two-thirds of survey respondents planned to age in their current homes and one-quarter were not sure. About 12 percent expected to move to another house. Here are some more survey findings.

Aging-in-Place Home Preferences

Top 10 Home Features for Aging in Place

1. High-speed Internet access
2. Washer and dryer in the home/unit
3. Storage space
4. Easy-open windows
5. Easily-to-use climate controls
6. Master bedroom on the first floor
7. Attached garage with door opener
8. Private patio, front and back porch
9. Bigger bathroom, on entry level
10. Grab bars in bathroom

Four Top Services for Aging in Place

- Exterior and outdoor maintenance
- Home repair services
- Housekeeping
- Health care services

Four Features Consumers Want, but Most Builders Don't Build

- Non-slip flooring
- Large medicine cabinet
- Master bedroom on 1st floor
- Kitchen cabinets a little lower

Green Living? Not a Major Concern for Baby Boomers

- 27 percent of buyers are concerned about environmental impact, but it's not an issue in the home purchase. 23 percent are not concerned.

- 37 percent want an eco-friendly home but would not pay more for it.

- 12 percent will pay up to 5 percent more for an environmentally friendly home if it saves a lot annually on utility costs.

- Top 3 most preferred green features: energy-saving appliances, solar heating, water filter system.

Universal Design Standards

Universal design is a method of making products and environs so that they are usable by all people to the greatest extent possible. Universal design features can make it likely for you to stay at ease and safe in your home on an independent basis and for a longer time. Such design is a growing trend in home building. Here's the concept:

The following list of features can be components of a universal house. The example is just part of a list of specs on the *Institute for Human Centered Design* website. I include it here to give you an idea of the model.

Entrances

- No steps at entrances

  - Making all home entrances stepless is best.

  - More than one stepless entrance is preferred.

  - At least one stepless entrance is essential; if only one, not through a garage or from a patio or deck.

- View of visitors for all people, including children and seated users

  - Sidelights,

  - Wide-angle viewers,

- TV monitors, and/or

- Windows in doors or nearby.

- A place to put packages while opening doors: built-in shelf, bench, or table with knee space below found on the outside next to the door.

- Weather protection shelter while unlocking and opening doors

  - Porch,

  - Stoop with roof,

  - Long roof overhang,

  - Awning, and/or

  - Carport.

- A way for visitors to communicate with residents

  - Lighted doorbell,

  - Intercom with portable telephone link, and/or

  - Hardwired intercom.

- Space at entry doors: minimum 5 ft. X 5 ft. level clear space on both inside and outside of entry door for maneuvering while opening or closing door (can be smaller if automatic power door is provided).

- Light for entry doors

- Focused light on lockset,

- General illumination for seeing visitors at night, and/or

- Motion detector controls that turn on lights when someone approaches the door, help end the problem of dark approaches to the home and add a sense of security.

Address house number: large, high contrast and put in a prominent place to be easy for friends and emergency personnel to find.

Get the picture? There are many sites, official and unofficial, where you can go to get as much detail as you will need on this subject. Use Google, or your favorite search engine, to find them.

Adapting a Home for Aging in Place

A builder trained to apply Universal Design standards to a remodeling project can work from the following checklists. Use them to make sure the remodel meets all your needs.

Bathroom

- Tub and shower controls offset

- Light in shower stall

- Shower stall with low or no threshold, trench drain

- Fold-down shower seat

- Hand-held showerhead with 6' hose

- Lift or transfer seat for bathtub

- Lower bathtub for easier access

- Grab bars at back and sides of shower, tub, and toilet, or wall-reinforcement for later installation

- Adapter to raise toilet seat 2½-3" higher than standard

- Turnaround and transfer space for walker or wheelchair (36" x 36")

- Knee space under sink and vanity

- Counters at sit-down height

- Emergency alert or call button

Faucets, Switches, Controls

- Temperature-controlled or anti-scald valves for faucets

- Lever faucet handles

- Easy-to-read, pushbutton controls

- Lever door handles

- Loop drawer handles

- Easy-to-read, programmable thermostat

- Rocker light switches at each room entry

- Lighted switches in bedrooms, bathrooms, and hallways

- Light switches at 42" from floor

- Electrical outlets 15" – 18" from floor

- Front controls on cooktop

Entry and Stairs

- At least one entry without stairs

- 36"-wide doorways with offset hinges

- Side window at entrance or lowered peephole

- Handrails on both sides of stairs

- Outside stair height below 4"

- Contrasting strip on stair edge

- Ramp slope of no more than 2" per 12" in length, 2" curbs, 5' landing at entrance

- Low (maximum ½" beveled) or no threshold

- No mats or throw rugs

- Exterior sensor light focused on door lock

- Surface inside doorway for placing packages

- Audible doorbell

- Flashing porch light

Kitchen

- Cabinets with pull-out shelves and turntables

- Wall cabinets set below (about 3") standard height

- Glass cabinet doors or open shelving

- Easy-to-grasp cabinet knobs, pulls, or loop handles

- Task lighting under cabinets

- Electric cooktop with front controls and hot-surface indicator

- Microwave at counter height

- Wall oven or side opening oven door at counter height

- Counter space for transferring items from refrigerator, oven, sink, and cooktop

- Contrasting color strip on counter edges

- Side-by-side refrigerator/freezer with adjustable upper shelves and pull-out lower shelves, or a freezer drawer on the bottom

- Raised dishwasher

- Variety in counter height – some at table height (30") – under-counter seated work area

- Gas sensor near gas appliances

Home Design and Layout

- Easy-open windows with low sills

- Color contrast between walls and floors, matte finish wall coverings

- Adequate, accessible storage

- Wide halls and doorways (interior doors and hinges can be removed)

- "Flex room" for family visits or live-in care provider

- Attached garage with opener or covered carport, room for wheelchair loading

- Smoke and carbon monoxide detectors

- Low-vision adaptations:

  - Anti-glare glass

  - Stick-on, tactile markers on controls

  - Contrasting color switch plates

  - Electrical-plug pullers

Home Care

- Low-maintenance exterior (vinyl siding) and landscaping

- Housekeeping service

- Repair service

- Security and emergency alert service

- Uncluttered, unobstructed exterior and interior pathways

- Easily accessible filters on HVAC units

- Central vacuum system

Converting a Second Home

A solid plan for turning a rental home into a retirement dwelling is to buy a second home and rent it aggressively using the rental income to offset as much of the mortgage and expense as possible. When you're ready to retire, you can sell your primary home and use the proceeds to refurbish the rental house, which then becomes your retirement residence. Or, you can sell both the primary and second house and use the proceeds to buy a new home.

If you're looking for someplace in anticipation of retirement, you should wisely consider how the home will fit your future lifestyle, income level, and savings. For example, will the property still be within your means on a retirement income?

Even if you are used to the area, all your time there may have been during the same season. Before you make a year-round commitment, especially if you are buying a home before you retire, you should visit the area during both peaks and offseason. Doing so gives you firsthand experience of off-season living. Factors to consider include:

- Will the weather be too cold or hot?

- Will off-season road conditions hinder access?

- Will peak-season traffic jams be tolerable?

- Will services and shopping facilities be open year-round?

- Will there always be something interesting to do?

- Will peak-season visitors be too noisy or unruly?

Aging in the Community Checklist

Aging in the Community – Checklist

Use this checklist to assess your community for aging in place.

Medical

- o Healthcare facilities, doctors, hospitals, clinics, experts

- o Prescription drug plans

- o Crisis services

Market

- o Range of housing options and prices

- o Resale value and appreciation prospects

Cost of living

- o Total costs

- o Utility costs – electricity, gas, water

- o Taxes – property, income, sales

Climate

- o Changes in season and climate changes

- o Chances of harmful storms and natural disasters

- o Environmental quality

- o Physical features: parks, coastlines, mountains, scenery

Transportation

o Transportation – public and private volunteer

o Roads

o Traffic volume

o Golf cart sales and service

o Airport nearness and airline service

o Parking

Services

o Shopping (quality, choice, ease)

o High-speed Internet access

o Restaurants (range of prices and types)

Community and Activities

o Public safety

o Planned communities

o Employment prospects

o Volunteer opportunities

o Popular events and hobbies

o Cultural and educational institutions

o Opportunities for civic engagement

Senior and Aging Services

o Concierge services

o Nutrition (meals on wheels)

o Senior-specific places, communities, facilities

o Aging and human services

o Independent living support

o Congregate, aided, skilled care, nursing home facilities

Fitness	Properties
o Workout programs o Pool, golf, spas, wellness facilities o Walking trails and paths	o Upkeep-free (no lawn care, snow removal) o Storage space o Alarms in bedroom/bathroom o Garage or parking o Square footage o Barrier-free – no thresholds, wide doors and hallways o No fall hazards o Age-restricted, age targeted, NORCs

Source: SRES® Student Manual V 2.2

TakeAways

- To age in place successfully, you need a plan.

- Know where you are on the aging scale to know what you need for staying put.

- Use checklists to assess your home and neighborhood for aging in place.

- Use Universal Design Standards if you modify your home.

Chapter 4

Independent Living

Whether aging in place or moving to a new home, the first phase of your shift most likely involves self-contained living. For many Baby Boomers, an age-targeted community is an answer to independent living. The features, social activities, and freedom from home care offer the liberty and safety you might be seeking.

The Housing Cycle

Most older folks stay in their own homes in their 70s and 80s. When they do move, they move closer to home and into smaller dwellings. Being close to adult children, who base their careers in the metro area, is a top concern.

There are mainly four stages of retirement and homeownership:

- **Upsize** Age 50. Pre- to early retirement. They want a large house with room for the grandchildren and other guests.

- **Downsize** Age 65. At this stage, the grandchildren are teenagers or in college and no longer want to spend spring or summer breaks with their grandparents. Adult children are involved in careers and do not have much time to visit either.

- **Half-back**: Age 70-75+. Health begins to fail. The spouse and friends may pass away, and community ties weaken. They move back home, or half-back, to be closer to children.

- **Last home**: Age 80-85+. The final move may entail selling the house and moving to senior communes which have a range of care. In other cases, they may need to move to an assisted living facility.

Here are your main choices for independent living:

Active-Adult Communities

These places welcome active retirees because they make the area eye-catching to other high-income retirees who add to the tax base and create few demands on services. Active-adult retirement communities come in a variety of forms:

- Single-family homes

- Attached homes, duplexes, townhomes

- Condos

- Manufactured and mobile homes in a park, real estate owned or leased – popular with "snowbirds"

- Cluster housing with large common areas, such as gardens, clubhouse, tennis courts, swimming pools, and community centers

- Subdivisions

- Cruise ship condos

Who buys into these communities? The Del Webb Company, the largest developer of U.S. retirement neighborhoods, says the active adult consumer profile is:

- Socially, physically, and philosophically active

- Technology-adept

- Looking to be surrounded by "people like me"

- More driven by lifestyle than the actual house

Though focused in the South and West, we find active adult communities across the country. Del Webb placed some of the newest of them close to metro areas for retirees who favor a city.

Active adult communities may offer a try-before-you-buy option for a short-term stay. Likely buyers have a chance to try out the features, get a feel for the atmosphere, meet other locals, and decide if it is a good fit for them.

They offer a range of social events, comforts, and activities to attract and serve people. Functions and features might include:

- Computer labs

- Health care programs

- Community center or clubhouse

- Social and leisure programs

- Hobby, fitness, and workshop facilities

- Support groups

- Libraries

- Continuing education programs

- Worship services, spiritual counseling

- Outside upkeep and referral services

- Restaurants and meal programs
- Cultural and arts programs
- Transportation on a schedule
- Gardening plots

A National Association of Home Builders research study found that the most wanted features in an active adult community are:

- Lakes
- Security
- Outdoor spaces
- Clubhouses
- Exercise rooms
- Business centers
- Public transportation
- Outdoor pools
- Walking and jogging trails

Even if residents don't use all the amenities, they do understand how they add value, especially if they own real estate there.

Seniors Apartments

According to the AARP, about 20 percent of seniors are renters. They are either always renters or former homeowners who sold their properties to become renters. Reasons for becoming renters include:

- Divorce (dividing equity)

- The inability to pay mortgage, taxes, insurance, upkeep

- Moving closer to family and grandchildren

- The desire to free up capital for investment income

- Freedom from home and garden upkeep

- Freedom to travel

Seniors-only apartments suit those who can take care of themselves, are relatively healthy, have enough funds to rent the apartment, and want to keep their independence and privacy. They offer social prospects, comfort, safety, and security, but no medical or custodial care. Some apartment buildings become de facto senior housing due to the age of the residents.

The apartments are usually small and easy to keep up. The design may include shower seats, handrails, and emergency alert devices. Residents may have access to recreation, transportation, and communal dining rooms.

Some senior apartments qualify as low-income housing and charge below-market rents based on a tenant's income. HUD subsidizes many of these apartments. States or community grants support others.

HUD guidelines require the spending of no more than 30 percent of the county's median income for housing. So, there may be a long waiting list to move into one of these places due to low turnover. An AARP report on subsidized housing for older renters found that there are, on average, nine hopefuls for every vacancy.

Cohousing

Cohousing communities are self-contained, planned neighborhoods of privately owned dwellings. They may be single-family or townhomes around a courtyard and community center. Most are small, typically 10-30 residences, and may be multi-generational or adult focused.

Cohousing projects look like any other clustered neighborhood on the outside. The accent on sharing and communal living distinguishes them. Shared meals prepared by community member volunteers and served several times a week in a common dining room are a distinctive feature. Another is decision-making by consensus.

The co-housing approach goes quite well with green living. Mission statements of these communities stress the wise use of resources and eco-friendly stewardship through sharing as a community value.

Adult-focused co-housing communities offer freedom and the privacy of a single-family home within a caring group of people. According to the Cohousing Association of the United States, the unique features of elder cohousing are:

- For new developments, future residents share in designing the area to meet their needs.

- The neighborhood design inspires a sense of community.

- Residents manage their communes and do much of the work needed to support the property.

- A homeowners' association directs the community with stress on decision-making by consent.

- The village and its services are not profit-making ventures or a source of income for its members.

Age-restricted Communities

Age-restricted communities provide a setting in which seniors can meet and make friends with people of the same age group and use features like swimming pools and clubhouses in a peaceful setting. But, for buyers who have always lived in a single-family home, getting used to limits can mean fine-tuning hopes.

You should always be aware of the rules and limits here. For instance, are pets allowed? How long can grandchildren and guests stay? Are there limits on children using facilities? Try to become aware of the rules and get to know the homeowners' associations, their officers, and staff.

Most age-restricted communities try to find a balance so that residents can enjoy both the neighborhood and the company of children and grandchildren. For example, grandchildren or young children can usually stay for up to several weeks, although the allowance varies widely from one facility to the other. However, residents may be grateful for the age limit that prevents an adult child from moving in with parents and thus dodges an awkward situation.

Your real estate agent should tell you if a property is age-restricted and that you will be expected to obey its rules. But, there is no duty to prove your age or eligibility.

Housing for Older Persons Act (HOPA)

The Housing for Older Persons Act (HOPA) allows age-restricted housing by carving out an exemption to the federal fair housing law ban against bias based on household status. For all levels of age limit, it is vital to note that the constraints apply to the tenants, not owners. Federal law sets forth two standards for age-restricted housing:

- **55+ housing**

  - At least one person aged 55 or older must occupy 80 percent of the units.

  - Residents under age 55 may occupy 20 percent of the units, at the most.

- **62+ housing**

  - All residents must be at least 62.

  - The facility must publish, and follow, policies that show the intent to provide housing for older persons.

  - Reliable surveys or affidavits must prove the residents' ages.

  - Guidelines do not require programs of planned activities for either 55+ or 62+ housing.

TakeAways

- There are four standard choices for independent living: Active-Adult Communities, Seniors Apartments, Cohousing, and Age-restricted Communities.

- People come up with new ideas all the time to improve on these choices. Stay up-to-date with what's new by joining the free Facebook group called **Living Decisions - Resources and Ideas for Later-in-Life**

Chapter 5

Housing Options for Assistance

W hen health or life settings change, living conditions might need to change. Homeowners, and their families, facing such a life shift want a living plan that supports privacy and freedom. They also want safety and security.

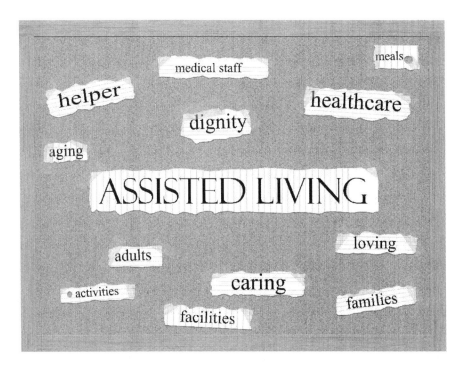

Choosing a proper level of care begins with assessing needs and skills. Typical, healthy aging does not need a medically oriented setting. However, because of falling strength, energy, mobility, and mental keenness a person may need help doing some daily activities.

When Is It Time to Make a Transition?

How you can handle the activities of daily living (ADLs) gives you a standard to know when it is the right time to make a change. The ADL list can also guide decisions about aging in place and in-home aid.

Activities of Daily Living

- Bathing

- Dressing

- Toileting

- Eating

- Transferring (e.g., moving from a bed to a chair)

- Maintaining continence

Up to age 85, most people report little or no difficulty with ADLs. About one-third of those who have ADL disability recover. After age 85 more than three-quarters report some degree of lasting limits.

Downsizing

When you need help with ADLs, it's probably time to downsize or at least declutter. The worst part of scaling down is sorting through and getting rid of a lifetime's buildup of stuff.

When health and safety risks outweigh staying in a home, it's time to find another living setting. But even when events are not at a crisis stage, you can run up against some challenging problems.

What stops people from making a change to a new living situation?

Obstacles

- Fear of change and loss of familiar routines that define and give meaning to daily life

- Fear of losing independence, control, and privacy

- Fear of being abandoned

- Fear of making a wrong and final decision

- Emotional attachment to a home or place – adult children may be more attached and resistant to breaking up a family home than their parents

- Resolve to hold on to a property so that heirs inherit it

- House locked financially or by maintenance issues

- Physical and mental limits

- Realization that a move may be to the last living situation and time left is short

- Stunned by the tasks involved in selling and moving

- Lack of family or a support network to help

- Belief that staying in the home is "living for free"

Can Family Help?

Families can be loving support when you need to make a change. Things are best when the elder is in control, and family gives support and elbow grease.

But family members may be unable to offer much help. They may also be too forceful and neglect the relatives' feelings, fears, and likings. There are times, though, when the family must step in and take control of the health and safety of the elder relative. You can use the following checklist for yourself or someone you're helping to downsize.

Downsizing Strategies

Space Planning	Sort into Categories	Assess Future Needs
• Subtract the square footage of the future home from the current house. Add in new square footage like a den, deck, or sunroom. • Measure furniture to be moved to ensure fit. • Ask if the facility – senior development, assisted living, continuing care – can provide space planning assistance.	Use various colors of Post-It Notes to help sort items into categories: • Move • Maybe – move and decide later • Sell – at auction, estate sale, yard sale • Give away – to family members or friends • Donate – to charitable organizations • Throw out	• Is it family-sized? • Items, like large camping tents, probably won't be needed. • Will it fit? • Compare size and square footage. A space planner can help. • Is it house-oriented? • If moving to a condo or townhouse, get rid of lawn mowers, snow blowers, and large gardening tools.

Throw-Out Strategies	Give Keepsakes to Kids	Managing Time

• Resist the "maybe we'll need it sometime" mindset. If you haven't touched it for more than a year, throw it away.
 	
• Consider if it's worth the cost and effort to pack, move, and unpack.
 	
• Still can't decide? Put it in a sealed, unlabeled, and dated box; if unopened a year later, throw it away, unopened.
	• Give childhood arts, crafts, and family photos to children; they may cherish them and use them to start their family traditions.
	
	• Receiving meaningful keepsakes may ease breaking emotional ties to the family home.
	
	• Ask children to sort items:
	  o Take now
	  o Take next time / Give away
	  o Throw away
		• Allow Time: Most downsizing projects take 2-3 months.
		
		• Start early: Begin the process before the house is listed. If it sells quickly, there will be less time for finishing the tasks.
		
		• Schedule: Set a plan by room, week, month, or other milestones.
		
		• Take Time: Spreading out the process makes it less emotionally wrenching.

Source: SRES® Student Manual V 2.2

Professional Assistance

Decluttering or downsizing is never easy. You might need a pro. If you do, look for a Certified Relocation and Transition Specialist (CRTS®). They can handle all the phases and tasks of downsizing, moving, or decluttering a senior's home. They can sort through all the stuff and arrange for getting rid of items. They can also prepare a space plan to make sure furniture will fit in a new living situation. They pack and unpack.

Fees may be on an hourly basis, by task, or for an entire project. Ask for a quote before committing. For more information about these experts go to *crtscertification.com.*

Decluttering

How to begin:

- Focus on safety first by removing fall and fire hazards.

- Start small and slow. Unless a deadline is looming, working at the elder's pace lessens the stress. Start small by cleaning a corner of a room or a tabletop.

- Remove dumped items at once so that they cannot be "resaved."

- Reorganizing items into categories – keep, sell, give away – may help start the process and make it easier to throw out things.

- Bargain and compromise over what to keep or discard. In may be okay to save the last couple of years of collected magazines and drop the earlier 10-20 years' worth.

- Photos of mementos may make it easier to let go of and disperse sentimental items to other family members.

- Safeguard valuables as you find them.

- When you complete the job, plan for maintenance, so the home doesn't become re-cluttered.

Hoarding

Hoarding often suggests dementia and impaired judgment. People with dementias are endlessly losing parts of their lives. Losing a meaningful role in life, an income, friends, family, or a good memory can have an impact on a person's need to 'keep things safe.'

People often start hoarding because they're afraid of getting robbed. Those with dementia may hide stuff for safekeeping, forget where they hid them, and blame others for stealing them. The Department of Environmental Geriatrics of Cornell University has a website about hoarding. It includes tips on dealing with clutter. Go to *environmentalgeriatrics.org*.

In some cases, out-of-control clutter could threaten your health and safety. Decluttering your home may allow you to go on living there. However, disorder may mean emotional or mental problems. You may need to move to a new living situation before you can finish the task. Here are your main choices:

Congregate Living

Congregate living is also called residential care, custodial care, or support housing. It combines self-contained life and space for yourself with round-the-clock care. This setting offers fully equipped private apartments. They range from one-room studios to two-bedroom units. They usually have common areas where tenants can mingle. Most units rent monthly.

They may supply cleaning and laundry service, transportation, and social events. Meals served in a common area dining room are usually included in monthly rental. Residents also have the choice to prepare meals in their apartments.

Most importantly, a staff person is always there to help the residents and check on their well-being. Medical care is not offered as a rule, although staff may help residents with self-medication.

Congregate facilities may have entry standards for age and abilities. They also may have rules for when a resident must transfer from them. For example, they may accept a resident in early stages of Alzheimer's. However, they may expect the person to move to a specialized institution in later stages.

Assisted Living

Assisted-living facilities provide a dwelling for those who need help with daily activities. They may help with cooking, housekeeping, and rides to the doctor or shopping. They may also assist with personal care such as bathing, dressing, and eating.

They are best suited for those who can walk and do not need nursing care but cannot live on their own. Living arrangements are usually a small apartment or a single or double room. They offer more privacy than a nursing home but less than congregate housing. Assisted-living facilities should provide:

- Laundry services

- Transportation

- Personal care

- Housekeeping

- Shopping

- Exercise classes (usually seated)

- Help with medicines

- Activities (social, religious, educational)

- Three meals daily with low-sodium, diabetic, and heart-healthy menus

When Is Assisted Living the Right Option?

Some signs that show a need for help include:

- Personal hygiene declines

- Replies to questions about well-being are passive

- A home that used to be neat becomes messy and dirty

- The refrigerator and pantry look empty, or a person relies too much on take-out food

- Stupor or fatigue replace being active

- Food left cooking on the stove, phone off the hook, bills unpaid, and drug doses skipped

Continuing Care Retirement Communities

Continuing care retirement communities (CCRCs) offer growing levels of care in one spot as your needs change. You can move between the housing setting and degrees of service within one community. You also gain the security of getting care through stages of aging.

Contracts for CCRCs

CCRCs typically run under one of the following types of contracts:

- **Life Care**: housing, residential services, amenities, and unlimited use of health care with no (or minimal) rise in fees. You usually pay a hefty entrance fee, but monthly payments don't increase.

- **Modified**: same services and comforts as Life Care, but they limit health care services. Fees increase when your care needs exceed built-in services.

- **Fee-for-Service**: same services and features as Life Care, but you pay for health care on an as-needed basis.

- **Rental**: a pay-as-you-go option and typically the least costly. It requires no entrance fee. You pay all health costs, but you are assured access to CCRC health care services.

Paying the CCRC entrance fee may use up a life's savings or proceeds from the sale of a home. Like any venture, you should make a careful evaluation of the facility, services, and its fiscal condition.

Have an attorney review the contract, especially the policy on return of deposits. Some CCRCs refund your deposit only when someone new buys in or a unit is reoccupied. In a slow market, you might have to wait for a home to sell before moving into the CCRC. You should know that the refund of a deposit can be delayed for years.

There are a few other things to consider carefully:

- their guidelines for forced transfers to higher levels of care

- how they treat life changes such as a marriage or death of a spouse

- their link to any religious or charitable group.

Evaluating Assisted-Living and Continuing Care Retirement Facilities

Go to these websites for guidelines and information:

- American Seniors Housing Association (ASHA), *seniorshousing.org*

- Commission on Accreditation of Rehabilitation Facilities – Continuing Care Accreditation Commission, *carf.org*

- Leading Age, *leadingage.org*

- Justice ln Aging, *nsclc.org*

- U.S. Government Accountability Office, *gao.gov*

Skilled Nursing Facilities

Skilled nursing facilities are what most of us call "nursing homes." They give round-the-clock care. Nursing homes have registered nurses, practical nurses, and nurses' aides. They can be freestanding or part of a CCRC.

There are two types of nursing home residents:

- Short-term patients who are getting over surgery or illness. Also, people needing physical therapy

- Long-term residents who cannot care for themselves and need more than they can get in an assisted-living facility

Most offer private and semi-private rooms. You would probably share bathrooms, either with roommates or between two private rooms. Unlike assisted living, nursing homes treat patients medically. Therefore, the program of social activities is usually minimal.

The range of quality is vast for these facilities. If you're thinking about a nursing home for someone's care, you should assess the service against several checklists. Visit the center without warning, and ask lots of questions. Residents of these services might be frail and suffer from mental issues or dementia.

However, nursing homes in most states must meet regulations and be open for regular inspection. They fulfill a need. Kind, caring, and cheerful staffs run many of them.

More Care Options

Elder Care

Elder care is an umbrella term for services offered to those needing help with activities of daily living. It covers a spectrum of services, from light to intensive care, at home or in assisted facilities. Eldercare includes services such as:

- Meals

- Socialization

- Personal attention

- Light housekeeping in the home

- Respite care

- Adult day care

- Transportation

- Visiting

- Telephone reassurance

- Caregiver support

- Emergency response

Program of All-Inclusive Care for the Elderly (PACE)

The government set up the PACE program so that states could give services to Medicare and Medicaid receivers. Not-for-profit concerns run the programs at the local level. They offer services at home and in assisted living and nursing home facilities. PACE providers receive monthly Medicare and Medicaid payments for each enrollee.

The concept of the PACE model is that it is better to serve elders and their families in the community when possible. The programs offer a range of care and services so that participants can live in their homes if possible.

PACE programs include home health care, meals on wheels, aid with activities of daily living, housekeeping, laundry, social work, and adult day care. Enrollment in a PACE program requires certification for nursing home care, but few recipients live in one. But if an enrollee does need a nursing home the PACE program manages payment for it and continues to direct care.

Shared Housing

Shared housing involves sharing a home with a roommate, in one's own home or that of another. Some community groups help with matching those who want to share their homes or find roommates.

Board and Care

Board and care are simple, small-scale assisted-living facilities for personal and custodial care. Some are in converted private homes, and they operate on an unofficial basis. They usually have just a few residents, typically 4 to 10. These are also known as foster care, group homes, or domiciliary homes. They are suited for those who cannot live alone and need support with activities of daily living but do not demand a nursing home setting. Long-term insurance policies may cover the expense.

Residential Care Facilities for the Elderly (RCFE)

RCFEs provide more freedom than a nursing home. They aid with activities of daily living but not medical care. However, staff may help residents take medications. RCFEs usually charge one basic price for a package. They add fees for extra services or reduce them for unused services.

Elder Cottage Housing Opportunity (ECHO)

The term Elder Cottage Housing Opportunity (ECHO) refers to a mobile or modular home placed on a single-family lot. When no longer needed, the ECHO unit is moved to another site and rented to another family. Before planning to put an ECHO unit on a property, you should check area zoning rules.

Accessory Units

Living spaces added to a single-family home go by various names – granny flat, mother-in-law flat, or accessory unit. They can be apartments within a home, flats over a garage, freestanding structures, or add-ons with a separate entrance. They are usually site-built and attached to the main house. They may still be useful after the elder tenant is no longer living or has moved to a care facility.

A legal second unit usually needs a separate entrance, bathroom, bedroom, and cooking space. You may have to get a zoning variance to have two in the same location. However, adding another living unit may improve the value of the primary home.

Senior Day Care and Senior Centers

Although not a form of housing, daycare facilities can help elders stay in their homes longer. They fill the gap when the caregiver must work during the day or needs a respite. Daycare centers offer supervision, usually a noon meal, social and educational events, and support groups. Some offer nursing and therapy services as well as health monitoring.

Respite Care

Respite care allows caretakers time off to recoup, handle other family matters, or get away for a while. In-home respite care workers come daily to stay in the home with the elder. An option is a short-term stay in an assisted-living facility if space is open. A brief visit may be possible and gives you a chance to try out the service without committing to move there for good.

Memory Care Facilities

Memory care facilities focus on the care of patients with Alzheimer's and other types of dementia. Congregate, assisted-living, or board and care may be fitting for residents in early stages. If the commune has no specialized unit, they may demand a move to another facility as the disease worsens. Families who want to care for an Alzheimer's patient at home need to bear in mind questions such as:

- Can the setting be made secure and safe?

- Do in-home respite services exist, such as nurses, home health aides, homemakers, and companions?

- Can the caregiver access respite care?

- Is there a senior adult day care facility available?

- Are there prospects for social contact, mental stimulation, and leisure for the Alzheimer's patient?

What Will Medicare or Medicaid Fund?

Medicare will not pay for custodial or long-term care in assisted-living facilities. Payment for assisted living is usually out-of-pocket. It won't pay for nursing home care that does not at once follow a hospital stay of more than three days. However, long-term care insurance may cover nursing home costs. Medicare also does not pay for any care received outside the United States.

Medicaid is a needs-based program with strict standards. You should view it as the payer of last resort. Medicaid may pay for stays in nursing homes (if the person meets a means test). However, it won't pay for assisted living and congregate facilities.

The federal government funds Medicaid, but states run it. And they have leeway in carrying out policy guidelines. The main rule for eligibility is that you cannot have liquid assets of more than $2,000 ($3,000 for couples in most states). This amount varies by state. If you plan to sell a house and enter a nursing home, Medicaid will not kick in until you spend down all liquid assets.

A person with home equity of $560,000 or more cannot get Medicaid. In a handful of states, that amount is $840,000. But the capital in a senior's home is exempt if a spouse, minor, or disabled child lives in the house. A home with less than $560,000 of equity doesn't count as an asset.

Payments from a reverse mortgage do not necessarily disqualify a Medicaid recipient. However, you must spend any income in the month in which you receive it. The rest is considered a liquid asset. If at any time you accrue $2,000 or more in liquid assets, you lose your eligibility.

Medicaid Look Back

A person cannot qualify for Medicaid by transferring or gifting assets to someone else, such as a child. There is a five-year look-back period for eligibility. You *must* be aware of this look-back rule if you plan to sell your house to enter a nursing home and expect Medicaid to cover the expense.

Medicaid Estate Recovery

When a Medicaid patient age 55 or older passes away, the state will seek to recover the amount paid on his or her behalf. They can reclaim costs for all Medicaid services provided, except Medicare cost-sharing paid on behalf of Medicare Savings Program beneficiaries.

States may impose liens to get the money back. Heirs are not required to use their funds to repay the debt. However, if the home is subject to an estate recovery lien, the heirs may want to use their resources to pay the Medicaid claim and keep the house. The state may also put liens on real property during the lifetime of an institutionalized Medicaid enrollee. They won't do that if one of these people lives in the home:

- the spouse

- child under age 21

- blind or disabled child of any age

- a sibling who has an equity interest in the house.

The states must remove the lien when the institution discharges the Medicaid enrollee.

States may not recover from the estate of a deceased Medicaid patient survived by a spouse, child under age 21, or blind or disabled child of any age. States might also waive estate recovery when it would cause an undue hardship.

TakeAways

- Know when to make a change from independent to assisted living. *Can you handle the activities of daily living* (ADLs)?

- Downsize or declutter with the help of friends, family, checklists, and professionals.

- There are many options available to you for assisted living:

  - Congregate Living

  - Assisted Living Facilities

  - Continuing Care Retirement Communities (CCRCs)

  - Skilled Nursing Facilities

    - Other options:

      - Elder Care

      - PACE

      - Shared Housing

      - Board and Care

      - Residential Care Facilities for the Elderly (RCFE)

      - Elder Cottage Housing Opportunities (ECHOs)

- Accessory Units

- Senior Day Care and Senior Centers

- Respite Care

- Memory Care Facilities

- Understand what Medicare or Medicaid will pay.

Chapter 6

Financing Options

In the U.S., more than 80 percent of the 50+ age group are homeowners. For many, the home is the biggest asset and the equity in it the chief source of net worth. Many homeowners have substantial capital through mortgage pay down and value appreciation. But, there is no doubt that the Great Recession took a big bite out of home equity and savings for retirees and near-retirees. Many have had to rethink retirement plans and dreams.

Do These Scenarios Sound Familiar?

- You would like to sell your house. However, you are waiting to get the right price, so you can pay cash for a new one and avoid mortgage payments.

- A loved one is about to lose a home to foreclosure. His fixed income hasn't kept up with the cost of living, and he can't afford the mortgage payments.

- You can't move from a declining neighborhood because the sale proceeds from the current home won't be enough to buy in a better area.

- Your family is struggling to find a way for your relative to stay safely in a long-time home. Her income isn't enough to pay for in-home help.

- You would like to buy a second home, but don't want the drain of mortgage payments.

Ask yourself this question: How can I use my home equity to support and improve the quality of my life, make it through the next change, or just stop mortgage payments?

Allow me to explore the reverse home mortgage with you. There have been so many TV commercials about this choice lately that it almost seems shady. However, I want to make you aware of the options. I also want to guide you to the proper professionals so that you can make sure this is a sound and safe choice for you.

The Reverse Home Mortgage — An Overview

The Reverse Home Mortgage, or home equity conversion mortgage (HECM), converts home equity into cash. Like a forward mortgage, your home secures the loan. It's known as a reverse home mortgage because a lender will return the money you paid in over the years plus appreciation. You retain the title and keep living in the home.

The payments you get add to the balance owed at the end of the loan. Interest adds up at a fixed or adjustable rate. But you will never owe more than the property is worth, nor can the lender seek access to other assets. The lender places a lien on the property. But if you live in and maintain the home, there is never any repayment due.

Events that trigger repayment include

- a move to another house as the primary dwelling

- permanent absence (12 months or more)

- a stated maturity date

- death of the last living homeowner

- sale of the property

- failure to pay taxes and insurance or make repairs

You may pay off the loan through sale of the property or prepayment at any time without penalty.

What Can a Reverse Home Mortgage Do?

A reverse mortgage can:

- Add to the amounts you get from Social Security, pension income or public aid.

- Postpone drawing Social Security, thus boosting the monthly payment.

- Give you an income you can't outlive.

- Stop mortgage payments.

- Prevent foreclosure.

- Pay for in-home care, medical expenses, and long-term care insurance.

- Help you prepare a home for aging in place.

- Pay off credit cards, debts, and mortgage debt.

- Buy a second home or a new home.

- Upsize, downsize, move to an active community, or move closer to the family.

Case Files

Buying a Second Home

Dorothy and Brad Linnell were active retirees. Dorothy had celebrated her 65th birthday and retirement. Brad, aged 70, retired three years earlier.

After Dorothy retired, they were looking forward to spending winters in a warmer climate. With many of their friends buying properties in Florida, they wanted to buy a second home close to their friends. Brad had a dream of traveling around the country in an RV while they both were in good health.

They had good pensions and income from 401(k) plans, but they wanted to use the equity in their current home instead of dipping into their savings. Their house was appraised at $532,000 and had no mortgage. Based on Dorothy's age, they qualified for an adjustable-rate reverse mortgage line of credit of $285,950.

In the first year, they used $190,000 to buy a three-bedroom condo in Fort Myers Florida. The remaining $95,950 line of credit was available for future expenses and maybe leasing an RV.

Stopping Mortgage Payments to Prevent Foreclosure

Henry Liang's children finally convinced him to retire at age 70. Henry and May, his wife, bought their ranch-style home 15 years earlier. May was in the early stages of multiple sclerosis when they bought the house, and they needed a one-level.

Henry's delayed retirement increased his Social Security benefit, but the printing company where he worked for 30 years was going bankrupt. The pension he counted on was going to be lost or greatly reduced.

He still owed $125,000 on his mortgage, and the monthly payment was $1,594. The appraised value was $358,000. Henry wanted to stay in his home but if he lost his pension it would be a real stretch to keep up the mortgage payments.

His children were dealing with job layoffs too, and his daughter asked if she and her husband could move in. Henry qualified for an adjustable-rate reverse mortgage that would pay off the mortgage balance on his home and give a first-year $21,000 line of credit, and $58,500 after the first year.

Henry became free of future mortgage payments. He could also afford the estimated cost of $10,000 to enclose a porch to increase the amount of living space.

Supplementing Income

Virginia Dwyer, aged 79 and widowed, was always on the go before rheumatoid arthritis affected her mobility and ability to drive. She wanted to stay in her home but had trouble keeping house and preparing meals. Her two sons lived nearby but had young families and demanding careers. They couldn't help her day-to-day.

Virginia valued her independence and the serenity of her home. If she moved into either son's house, she would be living under the same roof with teenagers.

Homemaker help for a couple of hours a day – for meals, grocery shopping, errands, light housekeeping, and trips to the doctor – would give enough support for her to stay safely at home but would cost almost $1,200 a month. Virginia's income decreased when her husband passed away, and then, with the expense of costly medications for her arthritis, it was difficult to afford the help she needed to stay put.

The house appraised for $510,000, which qualified her for an adjustable-rate reverse mortgage line of credit up to $300,472. She could withdraw as much as $172,480 in the first year. Virginia could then draw on the equity in her home to pay for homemaker help and prescription medicines as well as other expenses.

Types of Reverse Mortgages

HECM for Refinance

The HECM for refinancing may improve your life by fueling cash flow. The payout can be monthly, as needed, lump sum, or a blend of methods.

HECM for Purchase

The HECM for Purchase provides a lump sum for the purchase of a home.

HECM Line of Credit

A line of credit allows you to draw funds from the equity in the home as needed. The line of credit maintains a growth rate that will enable you to tap into more equity without refinancing. The amount gained through the growth rate is nontaxable income.

If there is a mortgage balance on a property, though, the mortgage balance must be paid off before the HECM takes effect. The reverse mortgage will pay all liens before the lender calculates your payout.

How is a reverse mortgage line of credit different from a regular home equity loan?

- The borrower pays interest only on the amount withdrawn, and the remaining line of credit grows at the same rate as withdrawals so that available credit increases.

- The HECM line of credit does not require repayment until the borrower sells, vacates the home, or passes away.

- The amount available cannot be frozen.

- A negative-equity situation cannot occur. The debtor, or heirs, will never owe more than the property is worth.

Which is Best – Fixed or Adjustable Rate?

You should compare the cost of the mortgage and funds from a line of credit to a fixed-rate lump sum. Which would be the best for you? A HECM counselor can offer printouts, called TALCs, showing yearly and total costs and payouts for all options.

A lump sum payout could exclude you from public benefits, such as Medicaid. However, that depends on state and program guidelines. You should consult your financial advisor, CPA, or elder law attorney before choosing this option.

Total Annual Loan Cost (TALC)

The total annual loan cost (TALC) statement shows the full loan cost over a period. Unlike an annual percentage rate (APR), the TALC adds in time and value gain.

The longer you live and the lower the appreciation rate, the more likely the balance will surpass your home's value. However, if appreciation is high and you live in the house for a short time, the real cost of the loan can be high.

Ask the HECM counselor or lender for TALC rate comparisons for various stages of the loan, rates, and loan types. Two drawbacks on the worth of a TALC are:

- It does not consider the added value in a growing line of credit.

- The lender bases the calculations on the life expectancy of one homeowner.

Summary of Reverse Mortgage Benefits

- Tapping built-up equity

The main advantage of a reverse mortgage is that you can draw the equity in your home to get fast cash, lifetime payments, or a line of credit.

- Lifetime income

Tenure payments give a monthly income that will continue even if you outlive the life-expectancy tables. You can live in the comfort and privacy of your own home with the safety of stable income.

- Nonrecourse financing

Neither you nor your heirs will ever owe more than the home is worth, even if the value declines or payouts exceed the value. The lender cannot seek other assets to make up for a shortfall. If you or your heirs try to sell the property in an arm's length (not to a relative) sale and the proceeds fall short, no mortgage balance is due. Mortgage insurance compensates the lender for a shortfall.

- Tax-free payouts

The IRS does not consider money borrowed through a reverse mortgage taxable income.

When Is a Reverse Mortgage Not a Good Idea?

If you are planning to move in one year or less, a HECM may not be a wise choice. The scenarios below offer cases of when it would not be in your best interest to use a reverse mortgage.

- If you have low equity or property value

When you don't have much investment in the property – less than 40 percent – or the property value is small. In this case, the amount you can get through a HECM probably won't offset the costs.

- If you have large assets

If you have a lot of other assets, you might want to think about using them first. However, using significant assets may involve fees, taxes, and penalties. It is often better to use the equity in the home than it is to spend down other assets.

- If you have short-term, small financial needs, or no compelling need

HECM costs outweigh the benefits if your needs are short-term or modest. It is usually not the best choice if you will likely need nursing home care soon.

The costs of a reverse mortgage are high. It is not "free" money. Don't consider a HECM if you don't have a compelling need to draw out the equity.

- High-risk, low-return investments

You may be taking a foolish risk when you spend HECM proceeds on a high-risk investment or one with a lower rate of return than that paid on the line of credit. Your rate of return ought to exceed the growth rate on the line of credit.

- If you are planning to pay for nursing home care, buying into a continuing care community, or buying new homes not ready for occupancy

Because of the residency requirement, a reverse mortgage cannot be used to buy into a CCRC or pay for a nursing home stay of more than 12 months. An exception occurs when one spouse continues to live in the home. The payout from a reverse mortgage could, however, be used to pay for long-term care insurance. The proceeds could cover a future nursing home stay. Newly constructed homes are eligible if occupied within 60 days.

The Verdict – Good or Bad for You?

You should not make a final decision based on the information here. Fortunately, you must receive counseling from a Certified Reverse Mortgage Professional to start the application process. Hopefully, though, you now have enough to decide if you should take that next step.

Family Issues

Your state of affairs, needs, wishes, and quality of life should be the key factors in using a reverse mortgage. But family members need to know how a HECM works and what their options are when the loan comes due. They might want to keep the property but can't pay it off or get a new mortgage. If they don't prepare for this in advance, it could cause family friction. They can, and should, take part in the counseling session.

A person holding a durable power of attorney or living trust can make the loan on behalf of the homeowner. An appointed conservator can do so as well.

A reverse mortgage is an option for homeowners who cannot make a move because of low income. Those waiting to "get the right price" may be motivated to go ahead with planned steps if they don't have to rely on the cash proceeds from sales.

What Do Heirs Receive?

When the last living homeowner passes away, the equity that's left in the property goes to the heirs, not the bank. But heirs must either pay off the loan to keep the home or sell it to access the equity. Heirs have three choices:

- sell (must be an arms-length sale) the house to pay off the debt

- pay off the debt from another source

- obtain a new forward mortgage on the home.

The heirs must meet mortgage underwriting criteria for a forward mortgage. If the house sells for less than the mortgage balance, FHA insurance compensates the lender for the difference.

If there are no heirs, the bank may take the home back and sell it. The estate may keep ownership of the property, but it must pay off the loan. Spending down the equity in the house, however, reduces the value for estate tax purposes.

Selling Your House as an Installment Sale

If you have a lot of equity in your property and don't need a lump sum payment from the sale, an installment sale is a choice that has tax benefits. You pay tax only on the amount received during the calendar year, instead of the entire amount. This spreads out the tax liability.

For tax purposes, each payment received distributes between ordinary income and capital gain. If the home sold qualifies for the IRC 121 Exclusion and the profit is under $500,000 (Married Filing Jointly) or $250,000 (Single), then only the interest accrued each year is taxed. The title may or may not pass to the buyer at the time of the installment sale, depending on state law.

You should get a down payment of about 20 percent and "carry back" the loan. The buyer should make regular payments, usually monthly.

You must receive at least one payment in the tax year after the sale. Older sellers should amortize the loan over 30 years, but call it due in 10-15 years. This structure ensures that the principal stays relatively intact and creates a good situation for the heirs.

TakeAways

- If you don't have enough money for retirement from investments, you'll have to get creative to live.

  - Visit the websites listed in this book's Resources section for help.

- A reverse mortgage is a possibility, but it is expensive.

  - This option calls for caution, family involvement, and careful analysis.

- Selling your house as an installment sale is another choice, but you must have a lot of equity in it.

Chapter 7

Tax Matters

In this section, we'll look at the most common tax issues of concern for Baby Boomer homeowners and retirees. Tax laws change all the time, though. When problems and concerns arise, you should seek the advice of experts.

Taxes on a Reverse Mortgage

Reverse mortgages are loan advances and not income. Therefore, the amount you receive is not subject to taxes. You cannot deduct interest expense accrued on a reverse mortgage until you pay the interest, which is usually when the mortgage is paid off.

Declaring a Principal Residence

Taxes can have an impact on retirees' choices of where to live. Those on fixed incomes fare better in states that have:

- low or no personal income tax

- little or no sales tax

- low real estate tax rates

For those who keep a home in more than one state, you must decide which one is your principal residence. The IRS states that you can have only one at a time. Your choice can have a big impact on income and real estate tax as well as how you split up property among heirs. For example, many states give a homestead exemption that offers some tax relief for seniors. Some states give a property tax deferral or freeze.

Here's how you can prove you live mainly in a specific state:

- Present an affidavit showing residency.

- Register to vote.

- Keep a record of how long you spent living there.

- Open a bank account.

- Join a church or temple.

- Get a driver's license.

- Pay a utility bill.

- File a tax return.

- Prepare a will that shows that address.

Capital Gains Tax on Sale of Principal Residences

- You pay no taxes on a capital gain of up to $250,000 if you are a single tax filer. If you're married filing jointly, you can have a capital gain of up to $500,000 and pay no tax. You must own the property and use it as a primary dwelling for at least two years out of five before the sale.

  - You can claim it repeatedly if you meet all the constraints.

- Widows can claim the full $500,000 if the sale occurs within two years of the death of a spouse and they have not remarried.

- Military and Foreign Service personnel on qualified active duty can suspend the five-year test period for up to 10 years.

- You can get an exemption if you must sell due to these events:

  - an illness or disability (your own or that of a family member for whose care you are in charge)

  - job relocation

  - specified sudden circumstances

Let's suppose you lived in a house as a primary home for one year before being disabled. You were then forced to sell the house to move to a nursing home. In that case, you would receive half the exemption: $125,000 for single, $250,000 for married filing jointly. A doctor must confirm the need for care.

Capital Gains Tax on Sale of Converted Second Homes

Sales of houses used as second homes are taxable. It is crucial to know the concept of nonqualified use when calculating the amount of taxable gain: it is any period the homeowner, or spouse, or former spouse didn't use the house as the main home.

Exceptions

- Anytime the home was used or owned before January 1, 2009 does not figure in the calculation. Therefore, there is a less adverse impact on long-time owned second homes.

- You do not include any part of the five-year period after the house is used as the primary home. This provision eases a tax burden on homeowners who move to a new house and have trouble selling the former main home due to a slow market.

- A brief absence, up to two years, due to changes in work, health, or unforeseen events.

Basis Step-Up for Heirs

Basis step-up is a central concept for transfer of property to heirs. Heirs receive the estate assets on a stepped-up basis of fair market value at the date of the decedent's death. So, if an heir sells an asset acquired from the estate before the asset further grows in worth, no capital gain tax is due on the sale. The stepped-up basis rule applies to real property included in the decedent's gross estate. In community property states, living spouses benefit from a stepped-up basis for both the inherited and their shares of community property.

The stepped-up basis rule does not apply to property acquired by the decedent by gift within one year of the date of death when the heir is the original donor or donor's spouse. This clause prevents using the rule to avoid the tax law by briefly gifting the property to someone who is very ill or old and having that person will it back. The decedent's basis in the property carries over to the heir.

Estate Tax Issues

The federal estate tax is assessed on the total value of all a decedent's assets more than a stated level. You can apply the entire worth to the lifetime exclusion amount of $5,600,000. A married couple can shield north of $11 million ($11.2 million) from federal estate and gift taxes.

The total value, or equity, of the estate does not include assets such as life insurance proceeds paid to another beneficiary or a home occupied by a living spouse. Therefore, the capital of the estate may or may not be subject to federal estate taxes. That depends on whether the assets of the estate exceed the lifetime exclusion amount.

Transfers of property between spouses, known as the marital deduction, are exempt even when one spouse passes away, except if the living spouse is not a U.S. citizen. If the value of the estate exceeds an amount offset by a tax credit, known as a unified credit, the excess amount is taxable. Under the current tax structure, only a small fraction of estates pays the estate tax, but compared to ordinary income and capital gains tax rates, the rates are quite high.

Same-Sex Spouses

A state that grants same-sex marriages treats legally married same-sex spouses as married for all federal tax purposes including estate tax. The ruling applies no matter where the couple lives. The decision does not apply to domestic partnerships.

Life Partners and Non-U.S. Citizen Spouses

The IRS does not allow a marital deduction for property left to a non-U.S. citizen spouse unless it passes through a qualified domestic trust. They may receive annual gifts of up to $148,000 from their citizen spouses without tax effects. But all a citizen spouse's assets are included in the gross estate including the share of a jointly owned principal dwelling.

Estate value more than the amount offset by the unified credit is taxable. The IRS rationalizes that a non-U.S. citizen living spouse may evade future taxes by leaving the U.S., moving assets out of the country, and renouncing residency.

Unmarried couples are not allowed to claim a marital deduction. They can make annual gifts to each other up to $15,000, but they cannot take the federal marital deduction for transfer of their estates.

Financial planners may tell life partners and spouses of non-U.S. citizens who own substantial assets to create a trust – usually, a qualified domestic trust (QDOT), to receive estate assets and manage the likely tax burden.

Gift and Generation-Skipping Tax

Gifting assets to planned heirs during life, instead of as a gift, moves holdings out of the gross estate. It also provides the givers the pleasure of giving during their lifetime and assures that assets go to certain people. You can make an annual gift to anyone, free of gift taxes or reporting, of up to $15,000 per person. Each spouse can give up to that amount for a total of $30,000 in a year. When a gift exceeds $15,000, the value of the award is based on the fair market value as of the date of the present and not on the donor's basis, even if it's an interest in real property.

You pay a gift tax if the gift exceeds $15,000, but very few donors ever actually pay it because they make the award during their life. Although you must file a gift tax return, you pay nothing out of pocket until the amassed amount of lifetime gifts exceeds the unified credit exclusion. Payment of medical costs or college tuition is not subject to gift tax if the payments are made straight to the institutions. These are called "direct transfers." The top gift tax rate is 40 percent.

Note: A common misconception about gifts is that any gift over the exclusion ($15,000) results in the payment of gift tax. This is not correct in 99.9 percent of cases since the gift value of more than $15,000 goes against the lifetime exclusion amount, which is $5,600,000.

A typical event is for a parent to make a gift of an interest in property to a child or other beneficiary to avoid probate. Signing over a title or adding a person to the title of real estate can have gift tax after-effects. Adding a person to the title of real estate and granting them half ownership and a survivorship interest will usually exceed the $15,000 annual limit. You should consult attorneys and tax advisors who are experts in estate planning on these matters.

A unified credit is used to offset cumulative tax liability for lifetime gifts, generation-skipping gifts and bequests, and estates. You can subtract the accrued taxes due on lifetime gifts from the estate tax credit. Any part of the unified credit not used to eliminate gifts or generation-skipping transfers can be used to reduce or get rid of the estate tax.

Gifts from grandparents to grandchildren can trigger generation-skipping transfer tax. Gifts made to heirs who are not direct offspring, such as the children of a life partner, can also trigger GST tax of 40 percent if the recipient is 37.5 years younger than the donor. You can use the unified credit for gift and estate tax for generation-skipping tax. If you intend to bypass your adult children and give high-value property to grandchildren, you should seek expert tax guidance.

Community Property

Almost a third of the U.S. lives in one of the community property states: Arizona, California, Idaho, Louisiana, Nevada, New Mexico, Texas, Washington, and Wisconsin. These states include some of the nation's fastest-growing urban areas as well as desired vacation home and retirement places. California, Arizona, and Texas alone account for more than 20 percent of the U.S. population. The tax laws define community property owners of real estate by the location of the property, not the home of the owner.

The central principle of community property is this: All property acquired during a marriage is assumed to be communal property with each spouse owning an equal share. The couple retains community property status even if they move to a common-law state. However, separate property transferred to a community property state keeps its independent status.

The income from community property is considered community property. In Texas, Louisiana, and Idaho even income from separate property is community property unless spouses plainly agree otherwise.

In the context of capital gains, community property status is vital. When one spouse passes away, both the deceased and the living spouse's share of the property receives a basis step-up to fair market value. The basis step-up resets the basis for the asset. If the surviving spouse sells the property, capital gains tax will be due only on the amount more than the stepped-up basis.

When a married couple owns greatly appreciated real estate, this basis adjustment can yield large tax savings for the living spouse. The IRS forgives all the capital gains tax that would be due because of the value appreciation during the couple's ownership of the asset jointly upon the death of one of the spouses. The property must be titled as community property, not joint ownership, and be included in the deceased spouse's estate to qualify for the basis step-up.

You can convert separately owned property to community property by gifting one-half of a spouse's separate assets to the other spouse. Gifts between spouses are neither taxable nor limited, except for non-U.S. citizen spouses. However, if the recipient spouse dies within one year of the grant and the property is passed back to the original donor, the basis of the gifted part will not be stepped up to fair market value.

Taxes on Social Security and Pension Income

If Social Security is a sole source of income, the IRS does not tax benefits because they do not exceed the base amount. But 50-85 percent of Social Security benefits are taxed if a recipient's income from other sources exceeds a base amount.

As a rule of thumb, add one-half of the total Social Security income received to all other income, including tax-exempt interest. If the total is more than the base amounts – $32,000 for a married couple filing jointly and $25,000 for single, head of household, widow/widower with dependents, or married filing separately – Social Security benefits are taxed as income.

Money from pension accounts, deferred compensation; traditional IRAs, and 401(k) plans are usually taxed because you make payments to them with pre-tax funds. The plus is that in many cases, the recipient is in a lower tax bracket during retirement than during working years.

Chapter 8

A Few General Legal Issues

Confidentiality Concerns

Often, above all in a crisis, a relative or child may make the first contact with us about these later-in-life choices for an elder parent. This exchange can raise some confidentiality issues. The REALTOR® Code of Ethics affirms our duty to maintain client confidentiality. The following items can lead to legal concerns:

If a relative or child makes the first contact . . .

We must always ask if the elder buyer or seller is aware of the conversation and a willing and informed participant in the matter. We also must find out if the family member has the legal right, such as a power of attorney, to conduct the real estate deal.

If title and identity are in doubt . . .

We'll take the extra step to find the actual title to the property and who has the say-so to rent or sell it. We'll make a check of tax records. We'll want to know the identity of the person who contacted us and the link to the elderly owner.

We'll ask for consent to share private information.

We must deal with the owner directly unless okayed to work with others, such as family members. We'll ask for, and record, an elder client's go-ahead to share business data with family members.

If family members are to be engaged . . .

A relative or caregiver can assist both the elderly homeowner and us by acting as a guide, interpreter, and helper. They can help an elder work through the emotional and real-world issues that may be involved in selling a home. We'll keep the relative up to date and provide copies of transaction documents.

Adult children don't always know . . .

Adult children may have little or no knowledge of the parent's financial affairs. Furthermore, children may be green when it comes to buying and selling real estate and lack market knowledge. We'll help you by spotting needed information and sources.

We'll provide information on options.

When the children live in another area or state, they may be unaware of care and community support services that could help an elderly parent stay in the home. We can help a family make choices by giving information and contacts and sharing examples of what other families have done.

We'll always be alert.

Unfortunately, even family members can have wrong motives and aims. We'll be on the lookout for fraud such as selling properties out from under elders. The REALTOR® Code of Ethics states that a REALTOR® is not bound by confidentiality if a crime is intended and can be foiled.

Selling Below Market

We may caution you when asked to list a home at a below-market price. Why do we do this? Consider this scenario:

The seller accepts a below-market offer to sell the house to a relative, and other family members question the deal.

The seller says, "This is how much I want. I just want a quick sale."

In that case, we would probably write a letter to our client saying that we're listing the property below market value. We would also prepare a Comparative Market Analysis showing the current value and ask the seller and buyer to sign it. We would keep all the papers justifying the asking price in our records. Such a tactic would, of course, allow us to market the property as a "best value in the community," with the assurance that we would have done *our* best to protect everyone concerned.

Power of Attorney

A power of attorney (POA) sanctions a person to act as a legal agent, an attorney-in-fact, for another and make binding choices in medical, legal, and financial matters. Authority can be boundless in scope and time or constrained to a precise time frame or individual decisions, such as medical care.

Setting up a power of attorney can be a simple process, but the language needed for certain types of powers of attorney can vary from state to state. Many websites offer POA forms for free or low cost, but they may not tailor them to your state.

Financial and healthcare bodies often prefer their documents because their lawyers have reviewed the details to ensure they are legally adequate for those organizations.

When having an older adult sign documents, it may be best to have a witness present who may sign a statement that they were present and confirm their relationship with the owner. A valid power of attorney requires notarization and perhaps the signatures of one or more witnesses.

A power of attorney may take effect right away, at some point in the future, or under certain stated conditions. States do not usually require registration of powers of attorney with one exception: real estate deals.

Power of Attorney Ends with Death

A power of attorney ends when the grantor passes away or becomes incapacitated. Upon death, an executor, named in the will or appointed by the court, assumes responsibility for solving estate and property matters as directed by the terms of the will. Court-issued letters testamentary allow an executor to transact estate business.

A durable power of attorney is different from an ordinary power of attorney in that it will survive the incapacity of the granter. It may, in fact, only come into effect upon the incapability.

Health Care Proxy

A power of attorney authorizing decisions about medical care, sometimes called a health care proxy, does not allow the holder to act on other matters. Completion of a durable power of attorney often goes with the creation of a living will, specifying limits on resuscitation or life support measures. But that power of attorney may be limited only to medical decisions and immediate financial needs. The health care proxy does not have the authority to sell or transfer property to heirs or handle estate matters.

Acceptance in Other States

Although states may accept powers of attorney granted in other states, details, such as the number of witnesses, can stall completion of their forms. When a POA must cross state lines or more than a few bodies are involved, several forms may be necessary to ensure that the lawful person can act. Having more than one is essential when real estate is concerned and the attorney-in-fact lives in another state – especially if the state requires registration of a real estate POA.

Spouses and Automatic Power of Attorney

A living spouse has the right to make decisions about jointly owned property with right of survivorship (joint tenancy or tenancy by the entirety) and manage jointly held bank accounts. But if one spouse becomes incapacitated, the other does not automatically have the power to dispose of property or make decisions about money matters. It may be necessary to petition for a court-appointed guardian when issues of competency or incapacity are involved.

Terminating a Power of Attorney

As noted above, a POA ends when the grantor passes away. But other conditions dismiss a power of attorney:

- Divorce (durable power may survive in some states)

- Inability of the designated person to assume the duties and no successor is named

- Invalidation by a court

- Revocation by the grantor

What If No Power of Attorney Exists?

Sometimes action must be taken to safeguard assets or complete a deal, but the person who has sanction to do so is no longer able or has passed away. When no one else is approved to act, someone may request the court to appoint a guardian or conservator to protect the interests of the incapacitated person or other involved parties.

Conservators, Guardians, and Executors

The courts may appoint a conservator or guardian with the mandate to manage the personal needs and money of the person who lacks legal capacity. Or the courts may appoint an executor to settle estate matters.

What is the difference?

- **Conservator**: chosen to manage property

- **Guardian**: named for the protection of a person or an estate

- **Executor**: a personal agent named in a will as in charge of carrying out the orders and wishes of the deceased

- **Administrator**: a court-appointed estate executor

Conservator

A conservator is selected to manage the assets of people who cannot make decisions. Although laws vary among states, the conservator usually needs court consent to sell real estate. The court may appoint the same person as conservator and guardian.

Guardian

A court-appointed guardian ensures that a person gets proper food, clothing, shelter, and medical care. A guardian for an estate manages financial affairs. The same individual can be a guardian for both the person and the estate. The spouse is usually the court's first choice; the second option is a child or relative. If a relation is not on hand and able, the court may appoint some other party or a public guardian.

A person is entitled to receive a copy of the application, be present at hearings, and be represented by an attorney if they are cited for guardianship. The party applying for custody must prove incapacity. In emergency cases, a court may appoint a temporary guardian if the person or property is in looming danger.

Executor

The executor accounts for all the assets of a person who passes away and makes sure heirs receive bequests per the orders in the testator's will. The executor also settles debts and taxes owed by the estate. An executor can usually sell real estate if needed to settle debts and pay expenses, like medical and funeral costs. The will, however, must explicitly allow the sale of real estate for any other purpose.

Who Cannot Be Appointed

People who cannot serve as guardians or conservators include:

- Minors

- Anyone involved in a lawsuit or adverse claim against the person or property or who owes a debt

- A nonresident without a resident agent

- Someone specifically eliminated in a will or designation of guardianship

When a Client Dies or Becomes Incapacitated

What happens if a client dies during a deal, the term of a listing, or after making an offer to buy?

Usually, if a seller passes away during the term of a listing, the power to market and sell the property per the listing contract expires. A fee may still be due to the listing agent if there was an accepted offer before the death.

If a buyer passes away, it does not necessarily cancel an accepted offer to buy. The buyer's agent may discuss the state of affairs with the listing agent and work out a settlement short of the estate buying the property. Once appointed, the buyer's agent or the executor of the estate may either complete the transaction or negotiate a contract close.

When a buyer or seller becomes incapacitated, it is a dimmer situation. Unless the person has executed a power of attorney authorizing another to handle legal matters, a court proceeding would be needed to name an agent to act on behalf of the buyer or seller.

Probate

The probate process ensures that all parties follow the intent of a decedent. Probate can last up to a year or longer and expenses can run as high as 10 percent of the estate. The actions are public record, and a court-appointed administrator may not be a relative. Probate is a court-ordered process, gives notices to creditors, and provides a means to settle protests by heirs and creditors.

Some assets pass to heirs outside of probate. For example, life insurance proceeds paid to a payee other than the estate itself are not subject to the probate process. Property titled as joint ownership with right of survivorship and community property with right of survivorship (where allowed) pass to the joint owner outside of probate. Assets held in a trust bypass probate.

Listing a Property in Probate

- The court decides the need or advantage of the sale.

- The sale may be ordered to pay debts and taxes.

- Publication of a sale notice is needed unless waived in the will.

- A personal representative signs the listing with the consent of the court.

- The court approves the amount of brokerage payment.

- A hearing must confirm the sale.

Life Estates and Trusts

A trust is an estate planning body that manages the use and distribution of assets. A trust formed during the owner's lifetime is a living trust; a trust set up upon the owner's death is called a testamentary trust.

A living trust holds assets during life and issues them at passing. A trust can be changed or revoked any time before death. It can also be irrevocable.

By keeping real estate in a trust, you can preserve the use of the home for yourself and control the final transfer to heirs without probate. Upon death, the trustee takes over, and the trust continues for the benefit of named heirs. A trust can also be used during the owner's lifetime to plan for possible incapacity and avoid the choosing of a conservator or guardian. Creation of the trust and transfer of assets to it are not a matter of public record.

The trust can hold real estate and pass it to heirs without the need for probate. This arrangement is useful for the heirs of a person who owns real property in another state because it avoids the hassles of going through a probate process in more than one state. In an era of blended families because of divorce and remarriage, a trust arrangement also ensures that estate assets go to the planned heirs.

Marital Trust, A/B Trust

Spouses can launch an A/B, or marital, trust to create a federal tax exemption, twice postponing tax on their estate. Each spouse puts his and her property into the trust. When the first spouse dies, his or her half of the assets goes to the heirs named in the trust, usually the couple's children, with the condition that the living spouse has a life estate, the right to use the property for life, and gets any income it produces. When the surviving spouse passes away, the property goes to the trust heirs. It is not part of the second spouse's estate for estate tax purposes.

Using this type of trust keeps the second spouse's taxable estate at half the size it would be if the property were left straight to the spouse. This kind of trust is also known as a marital life estate trust or credit shelter trust.

Note: Tax legislation referred to as the Deceased Spouse Unused Exclusion (DSUE) can do much the same as the A/B Trust.

The Elder Law Attorney

A lawyer who specializes in elder law helps elders and their families deal with pressing issues and plan for life shifts. Although this chapter has covered some problems that arise when a property owner passes away, an elder law specialist deals with a broader range of concerns. Traits that distinguish the elder law attorney are:

- **Life-focused**: stresses sustaining a long life

- **Integrated**: combines legal issues into the larger picture of maintaining independence and quality of life

- **Interdisciplinary**: partners with other professionals – real estate pros, social workers, health experts, financial planners – in a holistic approach

Certified Elder Law Attorney

The National Elder Law Foundation (NELF) offers a certification program for attorneys who focus on and devote a significant part of their practice to elder law. The American Bar Association approves the NELF certification. The foundation offers an online directory of certified attorneys.

NELF certification is voluntary, and many attorneys who are skilled and experienced in the field of elder law do not hold the certification. However, the CELA certification shows an investment in and commitment to the specialty.

Checklist: Selecting an Attorney

- Does the attorney have the know-how and a good track record in the area of law you need?

- Does the attorney explain legal terms?

- Will you feel relaxed working with the attorney and sharing private facts?

- Does the attorney pay attention, take notes, ask questions, and follow up on the points you bring up? Does the attorney return your calls in a reasonable time?

- Are the attorney's look and manner professional?

- Is the attorney willing to give references?

- Ask what schools the attorney graduated from; check credentials with the state bar association.

- Look at the order of the office. Does it look ordered and well run?

- Is the computer equipment up-to-date and a match for the staff?

- The office site is a good sign of rates to expect. Are the firm's costs reasonable? Are you paying for a name firm but getting the services of a law clerk? If an associate lawyer is working with you, is he or she managed by a senior attorney?

Hourly rates should not always be the only deciding factor. An attorney who has low hourly rates but lacks skill may need more time to complete a job and cost more in the long run than an attorney with higher hourly rates and the knowledge to do the job properly.

Chapter 9

Schemes and Scams

Cash As-Is

You may receive an as-is cash offer from an investor. Many times, these types of investors will offer around 30 cents on the dollar of a given property value. While it may be enticing for you to accept an all-cash offer, in many cases, this will not be the best choice available.

Deed Scams

If your property is free and clear of debt, you may be susceptible to a form of deed scam. A scammer will file a fraudulent deed and sell the home without your knowledge.

Cons

A con artist may try to persuade you to withdraw money from an account to prove that a bank teller is stealing money from depositors.

Another scam involves asking for bank account numbers and personal information by phone to "verify" information.

High-Pressure Sales

Boiler-room operations that sell living trusts may target you. You may be told to pay several hundred dollars or more for a package of preprinted forms.

High-pressure sales of home refinancing charge hefty service fees for needless home loans.

Phony Home Repairs

Con artists often appear after natural disasters like hurricanes. They pose as contractors and offer home repairs at "bargain" rates. The renovations are poor quality or never finished, and the contractors disappear with money paid in advance.

Identity Theft

Everybody is vulnerable to identity theft nowadays. Shred revealing documents.

Fraudulent Mortgage Notices

A sales pitch for refinancing or other products masquerades as an official document saying, "call for important information about your mortgage payment."

Another scheme is a phony "official notice" that a mortgage has been transferred and future payments should be sent to a fraudulent "lender" at a new address.

***

Ah, there are so many; and they are growing as technology improves. I could fill many more pages with them, but these are a few good examples. Suffice it to say, if anything ever sounds fishy, too good to be true, or if two and two don't make *four*, be careful.

Note: AARP has a great Scam-Tacking Map at https://action.aarp.org/site/SPageNavigator/FraudMap.html?

Conclusion

I hope I have made it clear that aging with dignity and peace of mind requires planning and research. How pressing your plans must be depends on where you are on the scale. The scale is not one of age itself but of mobility, energy, ailments, and other measures of how able you are to take care of yourself.

You may be at a point in life where retirement is less of an issue than merely surviving. If so, your focus must be on the research about aging in place, independent living, and housing options for aid.

If retirement is your biggest concern, then good for you. The chapter on 21st Century retirement won't tell you exactly where to go or what to do. However, the ideas I've presented might get you started.

Money, tax, and law are factors regardless of where you are on the scale, so I hope you dug into that. It is regrettable that these subjects are so dry and difficult to understand. I did my best to simplify them and point you to great resources for more help.

***

The bottom line is that you don't have to resign yourself to dying all alone in a nursing home. If you're having those thoughts, you're just one of the millions who have the fear.

I urge you to let go of that notion because there are more options along the way than you might have imagined. Use this book as a stepping stone to the resources listed on the next pages to preserve your dignity and find your peace of mind.

Resources

Name	Website
Aging in Place	
AgeInPlace.com	www.ageinplace.com
Aging in Place Technology Watch	www.ageinplacetech.com
Administration on Aging	www.aoa.gov
Fall Prevention Center of Excellence	www.homemods.org
National Aging in Place Council	www.ageinplace.org
Care Services	
National Adult Day Services Association	www.nadsa.org

Name	Website
Continuing Care Accreditation Commission	www.carf.org
Eldercare Locator	www.eldercare.gov
National PACE Association	www.npaonline.org
Environmental Geriatrics	www.environmentalgeriatrics.com
Finances	
Greenpath	www.greenpath.com
HECM Resources	www.hecmcounselors.org
Justice in Aging	www.nsclc.org
National Foundation for Credit Counseling	www.nfcc.org
National Reverse Mortgage Lenders	www.reversemortgage.org

Name	Website
Money Management International	www.moneymanagement.org
Fun	
Reminisce Magazine	www.reminisce.com
Trailer Life	www.trailerlife.com
Grand Times Magazine	www.grandtimes.com
General Information	
AARP	www.aarp.org
Senior Citizen Journal	www.seniorcitizenjournal.com
The Senior List	www.theseniorlist.com
U.S. Government Accountability Office	www.gao.gov

Name	Website
National Council on Aging	www.ncoa.org
Health	
HelpGuide.org	www.helpguide.org
Housing	
American Seniors Housing Association	www.seniorshousing.org
HUD FHA Reverse Mortgage for Seniors	www.hud.gov
Jobs	
Senior Job Bank	www.seniorjobbank.org
Making Transitions	
Caring Transitions	www.caringtransitions.com

Name	Website
Medicare and Medicaid	
Centers for Medicare and Medicaid Services	www.cms.hhs.gov
Moving	
MoveSeniors.com	www.moveseniors.com
National Association of Senior Move Managers	www.nasmm.org
Quality of Life	
American Society on Aging	www.asaging.org
Raising Grandchildren	
Raising Your Grandchildren	www.raisingyourgrandchildren.com

Real Estate	
Crossing a Bridge	www.crossingabridge.com
HomeFree	www.homefreeusa.org
Relationships	
Senior Friend Finder	www.seniorfriendfinder.com
Senior Match	www.seniormatch.com
Age Match	www.agematch.com
Retirement	
Retired Brains	www.retiredbrains.com
Support	
Neighborhood Reinvestment Corporation	www.neighborworks.org/homes-finances

Universal Design Standards	
Center for Universal Design	www.ncsu.edu/ncsu/design/cud
Leading Age	www.leadingage.org
Volunteering	
Volunteer Match	www.volunteermatch.org

Research Sources

Beyond 50.05, A Report to the Nation on Livable Communities

AARP Public Policy Institute, www.aarp.org

Growing Older in America: The Health and Retirement Study

National Institute on Aging, U.S. Department of Health and Human Services, www.nia.hih.gov

Work and Retirement Patterns for the G.I. Generation, Silent Generation, and Early Boomers: Thirty Years of Change

Urban Institute, www.urban.org

Older Americans, Continuing Care Retirement Communities Can Provide Benefits, but Not Without Some Risk

Report to the Chairman, Special Committee on Aging, U.S. Senate, GAO-10-611 June 2010, www.gao.gov

The NRMLA Guide to Aging in Place

Publications, www.nrmla.org

Older Adults and Social Media

www.pewinternet.org

Older Americans Key Indicators of Well-Being

Federal Interagency Forum on Aging-Related Statistics, www.agingstats.gov

Metlife Mature Marketing Institute Research Studies

www.metlife.com/mmi/research

MetLife Market Survey of Nursing Home, Assisted Living, Adult Day Services, and Home Care Costs

Aging in Place 2.0: Rethinking Solutions to the Home Care Challenge

Boomers: The Next 20 Years, Ecologies of Risk

Changing Attitudes, Changing Motives: The MetLife Study of How Aging Homeowners Use Reverse Mortgages

Encore Career Survey

Engaging the 21st Century Multi-Generational Workforce

Housing Trends Update for the 55+ Market

Livable Community Indicators for Sustainable Aging in Place

Meaning Really Matters: The MetLife Study on How Purpose is Recession-Proof and Age-Proof

About the Author

Raleigh R. Lee

After almost a decade in the real estate business, I was blessed to have become a member of the Seniors Real Estate Specialist® council. My mission is to help those in need at a time in their life when they need to "cross that bridge." The bridge may be retirement, assisted living, changing their home to age in place, or some other choice best for them.

SRES® gave me a vision, and that dream created this book and our partnership with about 15,000 SRES® (Seniors Real Estate Specialist®) agents across North America. We have working relationships with elder attorneys, remodeling experts, assisted living centers, certified moving specialists, people who specialize in decluttering, financial experts, counselors and coaches for senior citizens, and the like. We are committed to helping you with what may be the most significant living decision of your life, no matter where you are in the US or Canada.

I hope this book has touched you in some positive way.

97957519R00098

Made in the USA
Lexington, KY
02 September 2018